D0218750

*The Cambridge Introduction to*
## Edgar Allan Poe

Much remains uncertain about the life of Edgar Allan Poe, the mysterious author of one of the best-known American poems, "The Raven," the Gothic romance "The Fall of the House of Usher," and the first detective fiction, "The Murders in the Rue Morgue." This book provides a balanced overview of Poe's career and writings, resisting the tendency of many scholars to sensationalize the more enigmatic aspects of his life. Benjamin F. Fisher outlines Poe's experiments with a wide range of literary forms and genres, and shows how his fiction evolved from Gothic fantasy to plausible, sophisticated psychological fiction. Fisher makes new and fruitful connections within this diverse body of work, and offers analyses of the major works. The critical afterlife of Poe's work is charted, and the book includes a guide to further reading, making this a handy starting-point for students and readers new to Poe.

Benjamin F. Fisher is Professor of English at the University of Mississippi.

# The Cambridge Introduction to
# Edgar Allan Poe

BENJAMIN F. FISHER

CAMBRIDGE
UNIVERSITY PRESS

PRAIRIE STATE COLLEGE
LIBRARY

CAMBRIDGE UNIVERSITY PRESS
Cambridge, New York, Melbourne, Madrid, Cape Town, Singapore, São Paulo, Delhi

Cambridge University Press
The Edinburgh Building, Cambridge CB2 8RU, UK

Published in the United States of America by Cambridge University Press, New York

www.cambridge.org
Information on this title: www.cambridge.org/9780521676915

© Benjamin F. Fisher 2008

This publication is in copyright. Subject to statutory exception
and to the provisions of relevant collective licensing agreements,
no reproduction of any part may take place without
the written permission of Cambridge University Press.

First published 2008

Printed in the United Kingdom at the University Press, Cambridge

*A catalogue record for this publication is available from the British Library*

*Library of Congress Cataloguing in Publication data*
Fisher, Benjamin Franklin.
The Cambridge introduction to Edgar Allan Poe / Benjamin F. Fisher.
  p.   cm.
Includes bibliographical references and index.
ISBN 978-0-521-85967-7 – ISBN 978-0-521-67691-5 (pbk.)
1. Poe, Edgar Allan, 1809–1849 – Criticism and interpretation.    I. Title.
PS2638.F45    2008
818'.309 – dc22       2008028110

ISBN 978-0-521-85967-7 hardback
ISBN 978-0-521-67691-5 paperback

Cambridge University Press has no responsibility for the persistence or
accuracy of URLs for external or third-party internet websites referred to
in this publication and does not guarantee that any content on such
websites is, or will remain, accurate or appropriate.

# Contents

# Preface

This book is aimed at advanced high school and lower-level college/university students. It consists of chapter 1, "Life," in which the mythologies (often quite negative) that have grown up around Poe the person are avoided in favor of a factual account. Chapter 2, "Works," provides coverage of Poe's works and their place in the literature of the world. After all, what initially gained Poe widespread attention was his critical writings, an irony since during his teens and early twenties he intensely wanted to be regarded as a poet. An additional irony is that Poe very deliberately turned to the writing of fiction, chiefly short stories, which appeared in newspapers and literary magazines, because such wares had wide circulation and usually paid sooner and better than the process of turning copy into books tended to do. As scholars have discovered, some of Poe's works were copied from their original sources by newspapers in distant locales, or were pirated by British periodicals. Poe's fiction and some of his poems continue to be read, to be sure, as his most appealing imaginative writings. Because his critical ideas appeared mainly in reviews instead of in a single, extended book, they have, with few exceptions, not attracted a readership so large as that for the poems and tales. Great controversies enliven biographical and critical approaches to Poe and his writings, as will be apparent in the following pages. Chapter 2 treats "Contexts." Chapter 4 focuses on "Critical reception," followed by a "Guide to further reading."

# Abbreviations

E&R  *Edgar Allan Poe: Essays and Reviews*, ed. G. R. Thompson. New York: Library of America, 1984.

H  *The Complete Works of Edgar Allan Poe*, ed. James A. Harrison. 17 vols. New York: Thomas Y. Crowell, 1902; reprinted New York: AMS Press, 1965; reprinted (with "Introduction" by Floyd Stovall) New York: AMS Press, 1979.

M  *Collected Works of Edgar Allan Poe*, ed. Thomas Ollive Mabbott, with the assistance of Eleanor D. Kewer and Maureen Cobb Mabbott. 3 vols. Cambridge, Mass.: Belknap Press of Harvard University Press, 1968–78.

O  *The Letters of Edgar Allan Poe*, ed. John Ward Ostrom. rev. edn. New York: Gordian Press, 1966.

P  *Collected Writings of Edgar Allan Poe*, ed. Burton R. Pollin. 5 vols. Vol. 1 Boston: Twayne, 1981; vols. 2–5 New York: Gordian Press, 1985–97.

P&T  *Edgar Allan Poe: Poetry and Tales*, ed. Patrick F. Quinn. New York: Library of America, 1984.

# Chapter 1

# Life

___

What has been termed the "enigma" of Edgar Allan Poe remains very much with us, even though he died in 1849. Some aspects of this enigma, which amount to slanting the truth, or to outright lies, originated with Poe himself.[1] Others were supplied by persons who knew him, by others who supposed that they knew about his personal circumstances and career, or by still others who falsified the record because they took suspect "facts" at face value. Consequently, a "Poe legend" emerged, which retains widespread currency today. One may not exaggerate in remarking that a biography, brief or lengthy, of Poe is published nearly every year, although exceedingly few facts about his life and career have been discovered since the late 1930s/early 1940s, and much must remain speculative about that life. The most reliable biography continues to be Arthur H. Quinn's *Edgar Allan Poe: A Critical Biography*, which dates from 1941, but which as a factual narrative account of Poe's life maintains its value.

An introductory book about Poe, such as this, requires sensible biographical treatment. Much in his life was anything but sensational; more often it became downright drudging, but drudgery did not suppress or distort Poe's amazing creativity. Whether personal circumstances provided the mainspring in his creativity may, however, be questionable. Poe is often associated with the South because he spent most of his first twenty years in and around Richmond, Virginia. He was born, though, in Boston, Massachusetts, 7 October 1809, because his parents, David Poe, Jr. and Elizabeth Arnold Hopkins Poe, an emigrant from Great Britain, were traveling stage actors, who happened to be working in Boston when Edgar was born. Their older son, William Henry Leonard Poe, born 1807, had been left in the care of his father's parents, David Poe, Sr. and Elizabeth Cairnes Poe, Baltimore citizens. "General" Poe, as the grandfather was called because he had contributed his fortune to assist the Revolutionary War, was a well-known personage in that city.

Baptized just Edgar, this second child of David and Elizabeth Poe at the age of two years entered a world vastly different from that of itinerant actors. Elizabeth Poe's acting abilities surpassed her husband's, and, after the birth of a third child, Rosalie, in 1810, employment took her to Richmond, Virginia in the autumn of 1811. David Poe had earlier that year deserted his family, although the precise causes for his decamping have never been determined. Mrs. Poe became ill and died in December. Local citizens rallied to support the dying woman and, shortly, her orphaned children, Edgar and Rosalie. Taken into the home of Mr. and Mrs. William Mackenzie, Rosalie became known as Rosalie Mackenzie Poe and lived thereafter in the Washington, DC area. Edgar became the foster child (he was never adopted) of childless John and Frances Valentine Allan, Richmond dwellers. Scottish John Allan had emigrated to Richmond, where he operated a mercantile business in partnership with Charles Ellis. Edgar later signed himself "Edgar A. Poe" (the "Allan" part of his name is frequently misspelled). During his youth he was much indulged, chiefly by Mrs. Allan and her sister, Nancy Valentine, of whom Edgar retained fond memories.

Poe received such private schooling as was then deemed suitable for educating children in prosperous families, and during these early years he apparently maintained cordial relations with the Allans. In 1815 John Allan decided to travel to Great Britain to promote his firm's commercial interests. His family accompanied him, first to Scotland, then to England, where Edgar attended the Reverend John Bransby's Manor House School, at Stoke Newington, a rural area near London. The school would later figure in "William Wilson." Poe left no other reminiscences of his years in Great Britain; the Allan family returned to Richmond in 1820. There Poe studied for several years in the school of Joseph H. Clarke, then at another for what was essentially instruction in Classics and Mathematics. Poe in these years befriended Robert Stanard, whose mother, Jane Stith Stanard, is often cited as the inspiration of Poe's poem "To Helen," published in his *Poems* (1831).

Life for the Allans changed with the death of John Allan's uncle, William Galt, in 1825. Allan inherited immense wealth, and Edgar assumed that, as a foster son, the wealth would eventually pass to him. Allan philandered, however, fathering several illegitimate children, and those alliances were to prove disastrous for Edgar. Poe's own romantic attraction to Sarah Elmira Royster, a neighbor, was thwarted by her father, who may have considered the pair too young to marry. Their letters were intercepted, a situation of which Poe remained unaware until long after Elmira had married Alexander B. Shelton, a husband much older than she, and wealthy, who was approved by her father.

In 1826 Poe entered the University of Virginia, where he did well in Classics and Modern Languages. He also accrued high gambling debts because of Allan's parsimony in providing him funds, which lack of money much distressed Poe. Allan refused to pay Poe's debts, so the young man enlisted in the army as "Edgar A. Perry." He was stationed on Sullivan's Island, off the coast of South Carolina, a locale he would use later in "The Gold-Bug," one of his most popular stories. He was subsequently reassigned to the Boston area. His first book, *Tamerlane and Other Poems* (1827), published by Calvin S. Thomas of that city, read on the title page "By a Bostonian," perhaps to forestall identification of the author if the book was abusively reviewed.

That Poe chose to be a poet instead of preparing to join Allan's firm, that Poe's early poems too nearly resembled those of Byron and Shelley, and that his performance at the university displeased his foster father: these and other circumstances (Poe's possible awareness of Allan's affairs and resulting illegitimate children) worsened relations between the two men. The death of Frances Allan, plus Allan's remarriage and several more children, led to additional conflicts, as did Poe's second book, *Al Aaraaf, Tamerlane and Minor Poems* (1829), published in Baltimore by Hatch and Dunning. Allan did permit Poe to shift military activities so that the young man could matriculate into the military academy at West Point. Again Poe excelled as long as he saw fit to pursue the mandated regimen, but, disliking life in the Academy, he got himself court-martialed and expelled.

At West Point, Poe trained specifically as an artificer, one who makes bullets and other explosives. Such care as must be exercised, else explosive consequences occur, may account for Poe's careful and parallel structuring in many of his poems and fictions, which often move very carefully from low-key openings to sensational endings.[2] During his stay at West Point Poe prepared another volume entitled simply *Poems* (1831), published in New York City by Elam Bliss. This book was dedicated to the West Point cadets, whose expectations that it would contain comic poems aimed chiefly at activities and persons at the Academy led to their underwriting publication costs. Poe may have composed humorous takeoffs on local activities and persons while he remained at West Point, but the poetry as published embodied no mirth, running instead to visionary, idealistic, often gloomy substance. Alongside the Byronic "Tamerlane" and Shelleyean "Al Aaraaf" appeared "Irenë" (later revised as "The Sleeper"), a realistic poem depicting grief in the survivor of a beloved woman, as well as funeral customs of the era, and "To Helen," an exquisite lyric (the first of two Poe poems with that title).

Leaving West Point, Poe made his way into New York City, where he negotiated publication of his *Poems*, thence to Baltimore, where he joined others in the home of his grandmother, Elizabeth Poe, widowed and invalided, cared for by her daughter, Maria Poe Clemm. The household included Virginia and Henry, Mrs. Clemm's children, and Poe's older brother, who was ill and soon died. The family was extremely poor, having vainly attempted to obtain a pension from the federal government for Mrs. Poe because of her late husband's efforts for Revolutionary War causes. Edgar himself tried, unavailingly, to secure her such remuneration.[3] From the time he left the Allan household, Poe's major demon, so to speak, was poverty. More than any other cause, hardships and worries regarding scanty financial means troubled Poe's life.

Receiving no income and little renown from his poetry, but determined to pursue a career in authorship, Poe in the early 1830s shifted his talents to the writing of fiction. These years remain the most vague period in his life, but he evidently undertook an extensive-intensive course of familiarizing himself with what constituted best-selling short fiction, which then highlighted either horrifics, derived from antecedent Gothic tradition, or comic themes, or combinations of humor and horror. These features were especially noticeable in tales published by *Blackwood's Edinburgh Magazine*, though that periodical was not the sole purveyor of terror tales. Either from his desperate need for money or because he divined the nature of horror fiction, Poe initially created short stories which, like many of his poems, often, though not exclusively, feature a trajectory from fairly low-key openings to sensational denouements. Thus he adapted the popular terror tale, so prominent especially in *Blackwood's Edinburgh Magazine*.

Poe's first five published tales appeared anonymously in a newspaper, the Philadelphia *Saturday Courier*, during 1832. Poe entered a competition sponsored by the *Courier*, for the best tale, but the prize went to another. Given the imperfect copyright conditions at the time, Poe's works could be published without his consent or even his knowledge. The opening of the first one published, "Metzengerstein," may well characterize much in his creative writing: "Horror and fatality have been stalking abroad in all ages. Why then give a date to the story I have to tell?"[4] The narrator's thoughts might be Poe's own when he wrote fiction, because most of his tales, even when they contain comic elements, follow this paradigm.

Poe soon competed for another prize, sponsored by the Baltimore *Saturday Visiter*, a weekly newspaper, which offered money awards for the best poem and the best tale. The writings were submitted anonymously, and the judges were astonished upon discovering that they had awarded the prizes for poem and tale to Poe. They gave him the prize for the tale "MS. Found in a Bottle," but, thinking that the same writer should not take both prizes, they awarded John Hill Hewitt's "Song of the Winds" that for poetry. Since Hewitt was associated with the *Visiter*, Poe was angered at what he assumed was complicity; consequently he assaulted Hewitt, thus making an enemy who long outlived him, and who published reminiscences unflattering to Poe late in the nineteenth century.[5]

More important for Poe's literary career, one of the judges in the *Visiter* contest was John P. Kennedy, an established older writer, who became acquainted with and sympathetic to Poe's literary aspirations. Kennedy's influence led to the impoverished young writer's obtaining work on a new magazine owned by Thomas White, in Richmond, Virginia, the *Southern Literary Messenger*, and to the publication of some of Poe's tales in literary annuals and gift books. Thus Poe's career as author and literary critic commenced with what seemed to be a dynamic start. His critical opinions, set forth in many reviews he published in the *Messenger* and other magazines, won widespread notice in an era when the print media were gaining importance across the USA. Poe the critic often caustically responded to what he considered inferior writing, earning him the nickname "Tomahawk Man."

Among Poe's *Messenger* reviews, two doubtless engendered particularly intense and long-lasting hostility from the powerful literary establishment in New York City. Poe absolutely demolished a novel, *Norman Leslie*, by Theodore Sedgwick Fay, a prominent New York author; and he was no less virulent in evaluating Morris Mattson's novel *Paul Ulric* (both 1835). Poe accurately condemned both for bad writing, and he accused Mattson of plagiarizing Sir Walter Scott's *Anne of Geierstein*. These novels were published by the prestigious, powerful Harper and Brothers, in New York City, where both writers were important. Therefore Poe came rapidly into ill repute with persons such as Lewis Gaylord Clark, editor of the *Knickerbocker Magazine*, in the pages of which Clark later spared no effort to calumniate Poe. The "Paulding-Drayton Review" (1836), a sympathetic assessment of two pro-slavery books, has been erroneously ascribed to Poe, though the author was actually Nathaniel Beverley Tucker. That Poe would share the sentiments in this review is debatable; White insisted on publishing in the *Messenger* what he himself wished, and he cultivated Tucker's acquaintance.

Presuming on a steady income, Poe married Virginia Clemm, his cousin, in 1836, and provided a home for her and her widowed mother, but differences with White led to his leaving Richmond in 1837 to seek literary work in northern publishing centers. The Poes went first, briefly, to New York City, though their sojourn there and especially the year 1838 remain biographically unclear. *The Narrative of Arthur Gordon Pym*, the early chapters of which were published in the *Messenger* for January 1837, appeared in book form in 1838, published in New York by Harpers in July and in London by Wiley & Putnam in October. In September 1838 the Baltimore *American Museum* published "Ligeia," which Poe several times was to cite as his finest tale, and in November "How To Write a Blackwood Article" ("The Psyche Zenobia"); its sequel, "A Predicament" ("The Scythe of Time") also appeared there.

The Poes moved next to Philadelphia, where Edgar secured editorial work with *Burton's Gentleman's Magazine*, which published two of his finest tales in late 1839: "The Fall of the House of Usher" (September) and "William Wilson" (October). Poe also contemplated establishing his own literary periodical, the *Penn Magazine*, which project did not come to fruition. His two-volume hardcover *Tales of the Grotesque and Arabesque* (1839, but dated 1840), published by Lea & Blanchard, included mostly tales published earlier in periodicals, with little new material. As Vincent Buranelli notes, though, publication of this book constitutes "one of the great events in American letters."[6] Since *Tales of the Grotesque and Arabesque* contains some of Poe's finest work, Buranelli's statement is well taken. Poe's name was also given as author of *The Conchologist's First Book* (1839), a book about animal life. The book was actually the work of Peter S. Duval and Thomas Wyatt, though Poe lent his name and some editorial work for what was a new edition, cheaper than the original, published by Harpers, who declined to reprint, so the new edition was published in Philadelphia. Poe performed like service for Thomas Wyatt's *A Synopsis of Natural History* (1839), though he was not named as author.

Poe and Burton eventually quarreled, so Poe was discharged, but in November Burton sold his magazine to George R. Graham, who merged it with his own *Casket* to become *Graham's Magazine*, with Poe as editor. He continued to publish his own works in the magazine, notably "The Murders in the Rue Morgue" (1841), which proved to be the first of three tales centered in the investigations and revelations of a French amateur sleuth, Monsieur C. A. Dupin, whose exploits are narrated by an imperceptive, nameless narrator. These two furnish the model for Sherlock Holmes and Dr. Watson, as well as many other such pairs in the annals of crime fiction. This tale provided many other foundations that continue into the present-day detective story. Other notable tales from this time are "The Oval Portrait" (1842, as "Life in Death") and "The Masque of the Red Death" (1842, as "The Mask of the Red Death. A Fantasy"), and an important review of Nathaniel Hawthorne's *Twice-Told Tales* that same year. His renowned "solution" to Charles Dickens's novel *Barnaby Rudge* appeared in the *Saturday Evening Post* on 1 May, and another of his most important tales, "Eleonora," in *The Gift for 1842* (1841).

During these Philadelphia years Poe became well acquainted with literary circles and figures, including Henry B. Hirst, a writer/attorney, and Thomas Dunn English, a medical doctor/writer. A third writer, Frederick W. Thomas, also came to figure significantly in Poe's career desires. Poe had less than favorably reviewed Thomas's first novel, *Clinton Bradshaw* (1835), in the *Messenger*, but he later expressed a more favorable opinion of the novel, and the two men remained friendly. Thomas was to be instrumental in Poe's attempt to seek political office, at a time when, imagining that he had "written himself out," Poe considered other career options than literary work, during the administration of President John Tyler, though that endeavor came to naught.[7] Poe did not cease to write, however, and two of his notable tales, "The Mystery of Marie Rogêt" and "The Tell-Tale Heart," appeared respectively in *Snowden's Ladies Companion* (1842–43) and in a new, short-lived periodical, *The Pioneer* (1843), edited by James Russell Lowell.

Disagreements with Graham over content for the magazine led to Poe's resignation and temporary unemployment. During this time he went to interview with President John Tyler for a political post, with assistance from Frederick Thomas and Jesse Dow, who knew Tyler's son. Poe got drunk, however, thus ruining any chance for a presidential appointment. He contributed to Thomas C. Clarke's weekly mammoth newspaper, the *Saturday Museum*, where a biographical sketch of Poe by Hirst, with information supplied by Poe, appeared in February and was reprinted in March 1843. For a time, once again attempting to produce his own literary magazine, Poe negotiated with Clarke about that venture, but no publication ever saw light. Poe published "The Gold-Bug," yet another prize-winning tale, in the *Philadelphia Dollar Newspaper* (21 and 28 June). This tale was widely reprinted, was dramatized by Silas S. Steele, and became Poe's first genuine national success. He also negotiated with William H. Graham, brother of George R. Graham, to publish a series, *The Prose Romances of Edgar A. Poe*. "The Murders in the Rue Morgue" and "The Man That Was Used Up," a gruesome and a comic tale, appeared in pamphlet form, but no more parts followed. In late 1844 "The Purloined Letter" appeared in *The Gift for 1845*, and "Thou Art the Man," a parody of his detective – or, as he preferred, ratiocinative – tales, in *Godey's*.

In 1844 the Poe household relocated to New York, finally settling in rural Fordham, where Poe spent the remainder of his life. In 1842 Virginia began to display symptoms of tuberculosis, which resulted in her death in January 1847. Poe's career took an upward direction for several years, commencing with publication of what has become his best-known poem, "The Raven," in the New York City *Evening Mirror* (29 January 1845) and the *American Review* (February), continuing with his lecture "Poets of America," being honored with a biographical sketch by James Russell Lowell in *Graham's Magazine* (February), for which Poe himself supplied much of the information, and reaching a peak when he began to write for, then to edit/own, a new literary weekly, *The Broadway Journal*, which continued publication into early 1846. In assuming control he alienated a former owner, Charles F. Briggs, who would cruelly caricature him in a novel, *The Trippings of Tom Pepper* (1847). Poe also formed friendships with other writers, notably Frances S. Osgood, Nathaniel Parker Willis and Evert A. Duyckinck.

Poe's friendship with Duyckinck led to two volumes of his work appearing in Wiley & Putnam's "Library of America" Series, *Tales* (Summer 1845) and *The Raven and other Poems* (November, but dated 1846). Poe objected to the contents in the former volume, complaining that Duyckinck had selected the tales, twelve in all, and that he, Poe, would rather not have included all three of his Dupin stories and "The Gold-Bug," i.e. his ratiocinative tales. Nevertheless, the books were noticed. Combined with the attention given to "The Raven," which was frequently reprinted, these books promoted awareness of Poe throughout America. In England, too, Wiley and Putnam books enjoyed good sales, and several of Poe's writings had been circulating, beginning with the London branch of Wiley and Putnam's pirating *The Narrative of Arthur Gordon Pym*. *Bentley's Miscellany* during 1840 pirated "The Fall of the House of Usher" and "The Assignation" (using its earlier title, "The Visionary"), from *Tales of the Grotesque and Arabesque*, without crediting Poe's authorship. "The Facts in the Case of M. Valdemar," in several pirated reprints (and with a different title), caused a sensation in Great Britain, where readers could not distinguish what might have been scientifically verifiable information from fiction.

Several less pleasant events assisted in bringing Poe's reputation into question in America. Invited to read an original poem to the Boston Lyceum on 16 October 1845, Poe instead first spoke about poetry, then read "Al Aaraaf," which performance puzzled and outraged the audience and led to denunciations of him in the press. Poe responded in the *Broadway Journal*, stating that he had been drunk during the performance and that he had intentionally perpetrated a hoax upon his listeners. Poe's reputation sank lower when he became involved in scandalous rumors concerning letters written to him by Mrs. Osgood and by another New York writer, Mrs. Elizabeth Ellet, the latter attempting to capitalize on her acquaintance with him to further her own literary ambitions. A nasty encounter with Thomas Dunn English was just one result of the trouble started by Mrs. Ellet. English henceforth became a relentless enemy of Poe, defaming his writings and morals in columns of a comic periodical, the *John-Donkey*, and long afterward, in reminiscences in the *Independent*, English unfavorably portrayed long-dead Poe.

The demise of the *Broadway Journal* in January 1846, from financial losses, left Poe without a publication he could control, though he continued to write and bring out his works in other periodicals. One essay that has long retained influence, "The Philosophy of Composition," in *Graham's Magazine* (April 1846), purports to reveal his creative methods in "The Raven." Poe evidently wrote this essay to promote himself since his poem had attracted widespread attention, though many readers still overlook comic possibilities in the essay. Poe told Frederick Thomas that "the bird beat the bug ["The Gold-Bug," which had been popular] all hollow,"[8] and so he wanted to maintain the vitality of "The Raven," however he might.

Moreover, Poe did not have to visit graveyards to gain inspiration any more than he had to have himself buried alive (temporarily) in order to write such convincing tales as "The Cask of Amontillado," "Loss of Breath," "The Fall of the House of Usher" or his hoax on that theme, "The Premature Burial." Furthermore, that the death of a beautiful woman is the most poetic of all themes may involve wordplay on Poe's own name and career. The death of a beautiful woman being the most *Poe*-etic [emphasis mine] of all themes adds ironic implication to this oft quoted/cited dictum. Poe may have comprehended what he did well – though dying young women and men were popular literary characters in his era – and enjoyed insinuating wordplay into "The Philosophy of Composition." Like wordplay on his name occurs in the tale "Silence – A Fable," to be discussed in the section on fiction.

A different variety of humor characterized another cluster of Poe's writings, a series entitled "The Literati of New York City," which began in another popular magazine, *Godey's*, in May 1846. These were fairly satiric sketches of well-known writers, especially those who had earned Poe's disapprobation. Since several sketches contained unkind remarks about their subjects, Louis Godey ended the series with the sixth installment. Thomas Dunn English's hostile published response to Poe's article on him led to a lawsuit, decided in Poe's favor the next year. The "Literati" sketches did nothing to improve Poe's standing in the northeastern literary establishment, which began to ignore his submissions for publication.

Because of publishing difficulties, and with Virginia's illness worsening, Poe resorted to drinking, which continued after her death on 30 January 1847. Mrs. Clemm remained with Poe, managed the household, and mothered the bereft man. "Ulalume," one of Poe's greatest poems, was composed during this year. Any autobiographical intent is uncertain. Although Virginia's death may relate to the speaker's own sadness over the loss of Ulalume, the situation may also have little or no personal foundation. Poe's reiterated comment when theorizing about poetry, that the death of a beautiful woman was the most poetic of all themes, is relevant to "Ulalume" in one respect because of brief life expectancy during the nineteenth century. Poe's interests in astrology may also have motivated his writing of this poem, which appeared in December 1847.

In early 1848 Poe began to lecture on "The Universe," a topic he expanded into a book, *Eureka: A Prose Poem*, later that year. He also met Sarah Helen

Whitman, a poet, from Providence, Rhode Island, the "Helen" of his second poem "To Helen." They commenced a brief courtship, which ended either when Poe's drinking became too habitual or because he feigned drunkenness to break the engagement. He also befriended Mrs. Nancy Richmond, "Annie," of Lowell, Massachusetts, and planned a lecture to be delivered in October in that city, but no lecture was given. Poe wrote to Mrs. Richmond that he had taken a life-endangering dose of laudanum, an opium compound in popular use in Poe's lifetime. Whether he attempted suicide or even took the laudanum has never been determined. He may have fabricated the episode to play upon Mrs. Richmond's sympathies. Whatever the case, Poe prepared a lecture, which he delivered at the Earl House for members of the Providence Lyceum on 20 December 1848. This lecture was published as "The Poetic Principle," which appeared posthumously in *Sartain's Union Magazine* (1850).

The year 1849 was a busy one for Poe. *Graham's Magazine* and the *Messenger* brought out several of his works, but more of his writings appeared in the *Flag of Our Union*, a Boston weekly. Poe had no high regard for this periodical, but its generous payments kept him returning. Works inspired by the California gold rush, "Von Kempelen and His Discovery" (a hoax tale), "Eldorado" and "For Annie" (poems more positive in theme and tone than those one usually associates with Poe's poems), and the sardonic tale "Hop-Frog," were published in the *Flag*. Two more poems, "The Bells" and "Annabel Lee," were completed and sold to Sartain for the *Union Magazine*. Poe left Fordham for the South in late June, but stopped in Philadelphia, where he seems to have suffered delirium tremens from too much alcohol. Recovering, he went on to Richmond, where he renewed ties with old friends. He also became engaged to Elmira Shelton, his early sweetheart who was now a widow, though her children were not happy with this match. Poe lectured on "The Poetic Principle," once in Norfolk (14 September), then twice (17 and 24 September) in Richmond. He visited several times with John Daniel (editor of the *Richmond Examiner*, a newspaper), who agreed to publish revised versions of some of his poems.

Poe planned to return to Fordham, then marry. Subsequent events remain unclear because of conflicting testimonies from those who saw him during his final days in Richmond. He apparently left on a steamer for Baltimore on 27 September, after which no trace of his whereabouts can be established until 3 October, when he was found incoherent in a Baltimore tavern. His old friend Dr. Joseph E. Snodgrass and Henry Herring, Poe's uncle by marriage, took him to Washington Hospital, where he was attended by Dr. John J. Moran, and where he remained unconscious then delirious, until he died early on Sunday morning, 7 October. The precise causes of Poe's death have never been determined. Hypotheses run a gamut from stroke, to undiagnosed diabetes or hypoglycemia, to hydrophobia, to gradual poisoning from air pollution (caused by the then new technology of gas lighting, which released noxious fumes). So the man who wrote so frequently about mysteries continues even after death to spawn mysteries.

Neilson Poe, a cousin, managed the funeral attended by few: Poe was buried on Monday, 8 October, in the Poe family plot in Westminster Presbyterian Church graveyard in Baltimore. Mrs. Clemm did not learn of Poe's death until several days afterward. Several brief, complimentary obituaries appeared, along with a lengthy, maligning account by "Ludwig" (Rufus W. Griswold) in the *New York Tribune*, 9 October. Expanded, this defamatory account appeared in Griswold's edition of Poe's writings (1850–56), whence depiction of Poe as a well-nigh immoral, demonic personage has persisted in many quarters. Lewis Gaylord Clark, reviewing the Griswold edition, vilified Poe's character and literary abilities. George Gilfillan published an account, first in the London *Critic*, 1 March 1854, and reprinted on both sides of the Atlantic. Complimenting Poe the writer's analytic and imaginative abilities, Gilfillan harshly deplored what he considered his personal wickedness. Poe's advocates were quick to respond in what they hoped would be more temperate memoirs, those by Nathaniel Parker Willis, James Russell Lowell and Sarah Helen Whitman being among the more temperate. Other accounts, by admirers of more enthusiastic inclinations, often did as much to blur the truth about Poe as the scurrilous memoirs had. A full-length balanced biography was not to appear for almost a century.

# Contexts

Because Poe was so steeped in western literary tradition, and since so much of his adult life was inextricably intertwined with the Anglo-American literary marketplace, one must not overlook those important influences upon his life and writings. A late comic tale "The Literary Life of Thingum Bob, Esq." (1844) chronicles a writer-editor's career, which might well be a précis of Poe's own experiences: "I have indeed 'made history.' From the bright epoch which I now record, my actions – my works – are the property of mankind. They are familiar to the world." He goes on to tell how he acquired a literary periodical, and then a second and third, which he combined into one: *The Rowdy-Dow, Lollipop, Hum-Drum and Goosetherumfoodle.* Thingum continues: "Yes; I have made history. My fame is universal. It extends to the uttermost ends of the earth." To answer the question, "What is genius? [assuming that genius in an author is necessary to become successful]," he responds: "it is but *diligence* after all." Responding to an inquiry about of what such diligence consists, Thingum explains: "Look at *me*! – how I labored – how I toiled – how I wrote! Ye Gods, did I *not* write? I knew not the word 'ease'."

Thingum's single-mindedness is evident in spite of his purposes being thwarted, time and again: "And, through all, I – *wrote*. Through joy and through sorrow, I – *wrote*. Through hunger and through thirst, I – *wrote*.

Through good report and through ill report, I – *wrote*. Through sunshine and moonshine, I – *wrote*. *What* I wrote it is unnecessary to say. The *style!* – that was the thing" (*M* 3: 1145). To contextualize Thingum's words more accurately as they might serve for placement of Poe, we should not hesitate to acknowledge Poe's diligence – he did produce a large corpus; he also possessed imaginative genius. A "genius" is a "creator" or "begetter," and though Poe fathered no children he certainly "fathered" many first-rate literary works in several genres. From an early age he wanted to be a writer (for him that meant a poet), and he defied John Allan's hopes that he would enter the Allan business firm. Testimony to Poe's intense commitment to his chosen path, early and late, is strong. Occasionally he exaggerated the circumstances that lay behind his writings, for example in the "Preface" to *Tamerlane and Other Poems* (1827), his first book:

> The greater part of the Poems which compose this little volume, were
> written in the year 1821–2, when the author had not completed his
> fourteenth year. They were of course not intended for publication; why
> they are now published concerns no one but himself. Of the smaller
> pieces very little need be said: they perhaps savour too much of Egotism;
> but they were written by one too young to have any knowledge of the
> world but from his own breast . . . In Tamerlane, he has endeavoured to
> express the folly of even risking the best feelings of the heart at the
> shrine of Ambition. He is conscious that in this there are many faults,
> (besides that of the general character of the poem) which he flatters
> himself he could, with little trouble, have corrected, but unlike many of
> his predecessors, has been too fond of his early productions to amend
> them in his *old age*[1].

Poe concluded: "He will not say that he is indifferent as to the success of these Poems – it might stimulate him to other attempts – but he can safely assert that failure will not at all influence him in a resolution already adopted" (iv). From this first slim volume onward through the ensuing twenty-two years, Poe did continue to write, and to revise his poems and tales – with extreme care, regardless of his comic dismissiveness about improvements to the poems.

Even in this early Preface, as we know, Poe could not resist a touch of mirth. Unlike Anne Bradstreet or Emily Dickinson, he eagerly wished to publish his poems, and, for that matter, to publish much else that he was to write. In tandem with the comment that the poems had been written during early teenage years, the disclaimer about flaws in the contents of the book may have been made to forestall harsh criticism of his volume. Such an apologue would have kept good company with others of its kind that prefaced many other books by American writers. Poe must have soon quelled any reluctance to publish, and to revise his poems, as revealed in his letters written during 1829 to Isaac Lea, a Philadelphia publisher, John Neal, and John Allan, his foster father. These letters concern publication possibilities for a volume to contain "Al Aaraaf" and enough shorter poems to extend the book to appropriate length (*O* 18–32).

Throughout his career Poe would comment either that he knew he had published something that was not wholly satisfactory (by his or others' standards), or that whatever he had already published was inferior to some other work in progress or just completed. His early letters to John Pendleton Kennedy and others who might assist his plans contain sentiments indicative of this attentiveness to publication (*O* 53–57, 73–74, 76–79). Later in his career he complained to Philip Pendleton Cooke, a Virginia poet who had befriended him, that the volume of his *Tales* (1845) displeased him because Evert Duyckinck, editor at Wiley & Putnam, had chosen for a volume in that firm's "Library of American Books" just twelve from seventy of Poe's tales, including too many ratiocinative and "analytic" pieces and omitting "Ligeia," which Poe considered his best (*O* 327–30). Since "The Fall of the House of Usher," "The Black Cat" and "Lionizing" were among Duyckinck's selections, one must ponder Poe's veracity. Poe later wrote to Duyckinck, inquiring whether Wiley & Putnam would publish a second volume of his tales, "containing, for instance, 'Ligeia', which is undoubtedly the very best story I have written – besides 'Sheherazade' [*sic*], 'The Spectacles', 'Tarr and Fether,' etc." (*O* 309–10). If he sent one, Duyckinck's reply has not been discovered. Still later, when his professional career had sunk to some dreary lows, Poe wrote to his friend, Annie L. Richmond, about publication of "Hop-Frog" in the Boston weekly, *The Flag of Our Union*, which was "not a very respectable journal, perhaps, in a literary point of view, but one that pays as high prices as most of the magazines" (*O* 425). Poe was still attentive to being read and being paid. Ironically, the total literary income for his active working years, roughly late 1833 (when he won the cash prize for the best tale in the Baltimore *Saturday Visiter* contest) to 1849, amounted to slightly over 10,000 dollars, poverty wages even in those days. Nonetheless, and when his fortunes were not the brightest, Poe in early 1849 could still exhort his friend Frederick W. Thomas: "Depend upon it, after all . . . Literature is the most noble of professions. In fact, it is about the only one fit for a man. For my own part, there is no seducing me from the path. I shall be a *littérateur*, at least, all my life" (*O* 426–27). That he was.

# The historical context

Poe's life spanned approximately the first half of the nineteenth century. During those years much in the USA went forward in the name of progress and democracy. Poe found neither platform appealing because he was wary of what progress meant. With an eye to Jacksonian politics, he feared that mob rule would result from democratic ideals and practices. Although mob rule did not occur, fermentation over politics, slavery, industrial growth, education, economics, social life and relations with other nations repeatedly surfaced. Poe's reactions to such ferment surfaced at times in his reviews or, usually fairly coded by satire, in his fiction. Certainly none of these issues would have reinforced themes of ideal beauty in his poems. Poe's background in Classics also furnished him with inspirations in theme and form for his creative and critical writings.

Poe's poems and tales often "speak to" conditions in his day much more than what I have called the Poe legend seems to recognize. Poe's verse may devolve from Classical forms adapted to poetry in the English language; as do many of his themes. "To Helen" (1831) may epitomize Poe's use of Classical legendry. His education would have familiarized him with lore concerning Helen of Troy. Poe's observations about prosody are scattered throughout his criticism, especially in "The Rationale of Verse" (1848), Classical or Neo-classical underpinnings are strong in "Sonnet – To Science," his concept of plot and unified effect devolves from Aristotle, and many of the tales resemble the Classical dialogue in theme and form. "The Colloquy of Monos and Una," "The Conversation of Eiros and Charmion" or "The Cask of Amontillado" might be categorized as Poe's revivals of that ancient form. Even when there are not the two-person interchanges of speech neatly patterned as in these works, the methodology hovers over many of Poe's writings. Although the dialogue is usually thought of as a prose form, the verbal exchanges in "The Raven," "Lenore," "Ulalume" and "Eldorado" show likenesses to the dialogue, whatever may seem atypical. In Poe's writings the unusual does not mean the unrealistic, as readers of "Silence – A Fable," "The Raven" or "The Murders in the Rue Morgue" know.

Some obvious historical influences on Poe include works about archeological explorations, travel literature, biographies of historical figures such as Thomas Campbell's *Life* of Petrarch or accounts of the English statesman Sir Thomas More, treatises on animal–vegetable life interrelationships, old religious texts, the Bible, scientific or pseudo-scientific writings, Sir Thomas Browne's writing, newspaper columns, plus many more. When his professional schedule prevented his reading of entire works, he often found useful information in encyclopedic works such as Isaac Disraeli's *Curiosities of Literature*, or John Lemprière's Classical dictionary, or Jacob Bryant's works on ancient mythology. T. O. Mabbott's notes in *Collected Works of Edgar Allan Poe* (1968–78) record many more historical influences. Poe was of course fascinated with time concepts, whether time past ("Tamerlane," "The Coliseum," "The Pit and the Pendulum" or "Epimanes"), time present ("The Sleeper," "For Annie," "Eldorado," "The Man of the Crowd," the Dupin tales) and time future ("The Conversation of Eiros and Charmion," "The Colloquy of Monos and Una," "Mellonta Tauta"). Poe's curiosity seemed to be never ending, and the precise nature of how he found some of his source materials keeps providing impetus for investigation.[2] That he was far more cognizant of events in the world around him than the Poe legend often suggests is beyond question.[3]

## The American context

Casual readers have considered Poe's writings to be much more European than American in substance. That bias must give way, however, in the face of much that appears in his writings. First of all, despite his cosmopolitan outlook, Poe was an American whose only foreign travel occurred during the five years when John Allan took his family to England, where he wished to solidify his business ventures. Poe's knowledge or awareness of other nations came mainly from his reading, albeit immigrants may have given him some first-hand information in conversation. That he was far more aware of the contemporary America of his era is also demonstrable, contrary to certain trends of thought that would position him, dressed in threadbare black and with a sickly complexion, in a drafty, poorly illuminated, and generally shabby garret, raven on one shoulder, black cat on the other, scribbling down his latest personal paranoia into jog-trot verse or a terrifying story (in which he figures as the major character), all the while uncaring or ignorant about the real world outside. That image vanishes, however, when we read many of his works or when biographical accounts impress us with some aspect of his knowledge of his American world. Some have said that "The Gold-Bug" is Poe's only really American tale. That thinking, too, must yield in the face of such works as "Eldorado," which has been critiqued as a poem about the gold rush of 1848–49, which certainly excited many Americans. I have commented in the previous chapter about the Americanness in *Pym*, and others have also placed Poe as a natural in American authorship.

A literary character who in his American guise has attracted much critical attention in recent years, the trickster, may appear in many of Poe's writings.

Such a character may qualify as an unreliable narrator, but the important question to ponder in context of Poe's trickster is: Does he – and, saving "How to Write a Blackwood Article" and "A Predicament," the narrator is a "he" – deliberately mislead us or is he, and thus are we readers, unaware of what he might be relating? Poe's turning fiction writer took place at the very time when what has been called "Frontier," "Southwest" or "Old-South" humor was commanding great attention, and he shared many of its precepts. Not for nothing did he register admiration for A. B. Longstreet's *Georgia Scenes* (1835) in one of his earliest reviews. That volume of sketches includes as hallmarks of American humor passages of brutality, violence and sexism, though this last feature was more boldly handled by some others among these humorists, especially George Washington Harris in his Sut Lovingood yarns. Poe quickly assimilated these same themes into his fiction. Like these yarnspinners, Poe was alert to capitalize on publishing brief tales that initially seem to be supernatural stories, only to reveal at the end that the fantastic events have been nightmares or drunkards' reveries.[4]

Like many other American writers whose fortunes were not the most ample, Poe tried several times to secure a political office to ensure a steadier income than literary work provided. On 19 July 1838 he wrote to James Kirke Paulding, then Secretary of the Navy, asking whether a clerk position might be available. No position was offered, but several years later Poe again became hopeful of a political appointment from President John Tyler. Frederick W. Thomas and Jesse E. Dow, friends of Poe and of Tyler's son, encouraged Poe's application, and he himself applied to others, e.g. John Pendleton Kennedy, then in Congress, and Abel P. Upshur, who succeeded Paulding as Secretary of the Navy and was a friend of the President, but when he went to Washington, DC, anxiety led to his becoming intoxicated, and so he ruined his own chances for political office. Poe's politics may also have deterred such an appointment; his Whig outlook contrasted with Tyler's Virginia Democrat inclinations, despite Tyler's claiming to be a Whig to obtain the vice-presidency under William Henry Harrison. Poe's political aspirations were ill-fated. His attempt to secure some financial support for his Grandmother Poe likewise failed.[5]

American Transcendentalism, or what he construed as Transcendentalism, which was a cultural phenomenon much in the news during Poe's productive years, elicited only disapprobation from him, nor was he pleased by what he saw as Transcendental in the writings of Scottish Thomas Carlyle or the German Goethe and others. Since he admired directness and unity in writing, Poe disliked what he found as too diffuse and metaphysical in the works of Ralph Waldo Emerson, William Ellery Channing, the younger, and Margaret Fuller.

Characteristically, he never missed an opportunity to belittle their writings. In "Our Amateur Poets – Channing," in *Graham's* for August 1843, Poe accuses that author of taking notions of sublimity from Carlyle and Tennyson (Poe was inconsistent in commenting about Tennyson's poems), and then becoming too effusive in his written expression to the extent that he forgot good grammar and versification (*E&R* 459–72). Poe's hits at Emerson and Fuller may have resulted from what he considered the successes of the *Dial*, that periodical of Transcendentalism, with which Emerson's name was strongly associated, and Fuller's not wholly complimentary reviews of his *Tales* and *The Raven and Other Poems*.

Ironically, since American Transcendentalism was most prevalent in the northeastern USA, and since he was born in Boston, and to parents who might not be designated as Southerners, Poe is placed by many as a Southern writer. However, that he spent most of his life in Richmond, Virginia was one of those accidents of fate. Although he worked for the *Southern Literary Messenger*, and years later he downplayed the quality of J. R. Lowell's "A Fable for Critics" for scanting Southern authors, Poe really lived most of his literary career in or near Philadelphia and New York City. I contend too that, despite some opinions to the contrary, works like *Pym*, "The Murders in the Rue Morgue," "The Pit and the Pendulum," "The System of Dr. Tarr and Professor Fether" and "Hop-Frog" are not so imbued with any underlying paranoia about African or African-American slave uprisings as they are instinct with other, more significant purposes. One might say that Poe's only actual work with a Southern locale is "The Gold-Bug," which did flourish as one of his most popular works during his lifetime. Codes of honor and chivalry toward women notwithstanding, Poe's writings are no more distinctly Southern than, say, the fiction of Mary N. Murfree, a Tennessee author whose works appeared from the late 1870s into the 1920s, could be called a Northeastern or Western.

## The context of slavery

Poe apparently was no more pro-slavery than many other Americans in his era. That he may have undertaken the sale of a slave for Maria Clemm, his aunt, is possible; that his African-American characters are usually cast as stereotypical comic figures whose actions and speech would make them typical characters in much writing of the time is accurate. That Poe had to share the attitudes toward slavery that appeared in pages of the *Southern Literary Messenger* during his employment there is far less certain. Poe did not write the "Paulding-Drayton

Review," in the *Messenger* for April 1836, of two books that contained pro-slave sentiments, as was demonstrated decades ago, and ignored by several more recent writers on the topic of Poe and slavery. The writer of that review was Beverly Tucker, who contributed several articles to the *Messenger*, and whose sentiments pleased White – and White's was the final word on what did and what did not go into the *Messenger*. Whether Poe endorsed the opinions of Tucker or those of Drayton and Paulding, we will probably never know. That Poe could have observed the lives of African-American slaves and that he could have gleaned information, had he desired, from his reading or from word of mouth is beyond question. Whether he chose to encode aspects of those lives within his writings, or whether he chose to do so in accordance with what some later readers of his works have argued, is not so certain. The appearances of apes or apelike characters in his fiction is also open to question in regard to any resemblances to African-Americans.

## Gender and sexuality

I shall comment later, in chapter 3, on Poe's writings in which masculinity and femininity seem to intertwine, and where, for the most part, tragedies result from imbalances created by the male protagonist, whose attempts to suppress what we would consider a feminine presence or component in the self are disastrous. Poe's early poem "The Sleeper" gives some indication of such disturbances, although the lady's corpse does not return to wreak vengeance on a patriarchal survivor. Nevertheless, her presence in his thoughts, corpse though she is, stimulates his emotions, all of which relate to her, and the narrator's mindset in "Berenice" resembles that of the speaker in this poem. Later tales of a woman's presence haunting her survivor, who has in whatever way killed her, become more insistent in arousing terror in the male protagonist, because of his ill treatment of the female in question, culminating with the death scene in "The Fall of the House of Usher." The late poems "The Raven" and "Ulalume" are artistic replays of such relationships, though they feature none of the disgusting horror that may repel some readers of the tales about women. *Pym* presents intriguing masculine/feminine issues, though the conclusion strongly suggests that Arthur Pym must integrate with femininity to achieve maturity, astonishing though his meeting with a female Other or counterpart may initially be. A counterpointing tale, "Hop-Frog," does not position a male protagonist against a female antagonist who is dead. Instead, Poe's using the dual efforts of Hop-Frog and Tripetta against the tyrannical, repulsive king and his ministers may indicate that Poe's imagination was beginning to take a new direction. He had, of course, earlier portrayed a situation where a third person misunderstood the nature of a pair of lovers, and in this respect "The Assignation" adumbrates not only Poe's other tales about the death of a beautiful woman, but also the slight deviations in technique for treating that theme in *Pym* and "Hop-Frog." Once again we realize that Poe's art is not wholly of a piece, but that he created variations on a theme.

Sexuality is evident in some of Poe's works, although since he was a Victorian gentleman it is certainly not so overt as, say, that in George Lippard's sensational novel *The Quaker City* (1844–45) or Melville's *Typee* (1846). There are hints that Tamerlane's early love affair involved sex, but "The Assignation" and "The Mystery of Marie Rogêt" offer the most sexually oriented of Poe's writings, with the triangular relationship in the former and a botched abortion figuring in the latter. Some readers have speculated that sexual insinuations underlie "Loss of Breath" and "Lionizing," and a more recent reading of "The Murders in the Rue Morgue" offers an interesting and plausible hypothesis about prostitution (in Paris) and the sailor, with like suggestions concerning prostitution in "The Mystery of Marie Rogêt,"[6] though one cannot go beyond speculation in treating these possibilities, no matter how intriguing they are. Although prostitution may not be the issue, "The Purloined Letter," too, holds out possibilities that what the Minister D—knows about the great lady he contemplates blackmailing relates to illicit sex.

## The graphic context

Other critics have established Poe's "flaneur" characters firmly within urban contexts, and I shall examine this in more detail below. Poe's protagonists consistently look at what visually looms around them, though they do not always recognize the entire significances in what they see: witness the narrator in "The Assignation," who assuredly has "visionary" propensities, but whose vision is confined to the tangible and sensual, unlike the vision of the Marchesa and her paramour, who look to a better love (sex they've already enjoyed) in eternity. The art–life bondings in the tale enrich the eternal life implications because art, in this tale and in general terms, is often considered imperishable. A gloss on Poe's theme in "The Assignation" may be found in Dante Gabriel Rossetti's "The Sonnet" (1881): we read there that a sonnet is "a moment's monument/ Memorial to the soul's eternity for one dead, deathless hour." The flaneur in "The Assignation" does pictorialize urban scenes, but so do the narrators in "How To Write a Blackwood Article" and "A Predicament," "The Purloined Letter," "William Wilson," "The Sphinx" and "The Cask of

Amontillado," or, among Poe's poems, in "The Coliseum" and "The City in the Sea."

Conversely, rural locales interest the onlooker character in works like "The Mystery of Marie Rogêt" (which draws on rural and urban scenes), "The Fall of the House of Usher," *Pym*, "The Masque of the Red Death," "The Island of the Fay," "The Valley of Unrest" and "Dream-Land," not to mention the Dialogue tales about existence in the afterlife. Moreover, we might think of the flaneur while reading "To Helen" (1831) because the speaker mentions geographical phenomena and, it seems, the world of his mind, if the poem represents his mental reflections, even when he beholds the interior scene. He also looks back into time, alluding to Greece and Rome.

That Poe's flaneurs often miss the underlying importance in what they see makes the works all the more enjoyable for readers, reinforcing the adage that the eye is window to the mind. Poe's narrators seldom get beyond seeing what is immediately in front of them, what is tangible. We should keep in mind that the flaneurs' visions bear out what was surely Poe's personal thought, put into the mouth of Mr. Blackwood, "Sensations are the great things after all," emphasizing that she "pay minute attention to the sensations" – to create forcible writing (*M* 2: 340). Forcible writing is consistent with Poe's commendation for plot. Experimenting, as was his wont, Poe carried the flaneur character into circumstances and literary forms not usually considered in flaneur contexts. Poe's experiments with this character become daring "graphicality," to use a word that he coined when complimenting Fuller's descriptions in *Summer on the Lakes* (*E&R* 1173).[7]

## The urban context

Like Charles Dickens in England, Poe may be one of the first American writers to put city locale to effective literary uses, a natural tendency in a writer who spent most of his life in or near cities. Of course Charles Brockden Brown had used urban environs in *Arthur Mervyn* (1799), delineating in part how a yellow fever epidemic can speedily ravage city dwellers. Many other American writers seemed to flinch from using urban motifs, giving readers an impression that rural life was preferable and that cities were to be avoided as much as possible because they were hotbeds of insanitary conditions, violence and crime. To many, the pace of urban life was too accelerated for comfortable, pleasant living. Poe was, however, the first American to use urban environs as centers of great interest to his characters (and, presumably, to his readers). His early "A Tale of Jerusalem" was set in that city when it was besieged, but the necessity for suitable food in that tale, comic though its theme was, might suggest Poe's being prescient about urban food shortages in time to come, and the same difficulty may be reflected in "King Pest." Cities' vastness made perfect settings for crime and mystery, and Poe's handling of such effects contributes to the interest in "The Murders in the Rue Morgue," "The Purloined Letter," "The City in the Sea," "The Man of the Crowd," "The Assignation" and "The Cask of Amontillado." As one who is also an urbanite, Ligeia may possess knowledge of intellectual and emotional life that surpasses her husband's. His removing Rowena, his second bride, to an isolated, unpleasant rural home may indicate Poe's taking a leaf from the Frontier humorists. His narrator's uncouth, almost savage, disposition seems very like that of one unused to civilized life. One wonders whether there are any servants in the home to which he takes Rowena, just as one wonders where the servants have gone when Madeline Usher is taken down into the sub-cellar of the family mansion. The live burial motifs in both tales may be all too understandable, supervised as they are by the narrator in "Ligeia" and Roderick Usher.

## The medical-scientific context

Epidemic illness was not unfamiliar in American cities, and sound evidence points to Poe's knowing about actual epidemics as an inspiration for "The Masque of the Red Death," though "Shadow – A Parable," may devolve from Poe's reading of Gibbon's *Decline and Fall of the Roman Empire* and, perhaps, other historical sources (*M* 2: 191–92). Poe's medical interests are apparent in "King Pest," the mesmeric tales, "Berenice," "Morella," "Ligeia," "The Fall of the House of Usher," "Eleonora" and "The Mystery of Marie Rogêt." Mental illness proper informs "The System of Dr. Tarr and Professor Fether" and "The Tell-Tale Heart," *Pym* and "The Sphinx," as well as various poems. Nearly all of Poe's protagonists evince paranoias, and some also power mania.

Medical science in Poe's era was just beginning to take strides away from superstition and folksiness. Poe's alertness to medical subjects is responsible for the galvanic battery shocks in several tales, and of course he knew first-hand the symptoms of tuberculosis and of paralytic stroke. Ramifications of medical science are evident in the live burial motifs that some readers think are so dear to Poe, not knowing that fear of live burial was not a product of literary Gothicism. The sensational aspects of premature burial caused very real uneasiness in actual life, because when embalming was not mandatory one could, for example, enter a death-like trance and actually be interred as if dead. There are newspaper accounts from as late as the 1920s that address the topic.

So Poe wrote with knowledge of very real possibilities when he composed live burial situations. In that respect he rose far above the average writer of Gothic fiction, because the latter wanted to titillate readers with lurid details while Poe comprehended the greater realities in such terrifying occurrences, and that they had rich symbolic value.

Accounts of medical science and scientific explorations were eagerly read, and not just in America, during Poe's lifetime. The technological components of the expeditions also aroused curiosity, though Poe was not always accurate in presenting such material. "MS. Found in a Bottle" and "A Descent into the Maelstrom" present details about sailing vessels, and the narrator in "A Descent" gives a scientific explanation for the motion of the whirlpool. Pym's sometimes extended accounts of what purports to be factual information, "The Cask of Amontillado" and "Hop-Frog," essays like "Street Paving," and even Poe's cryptographic writings, display his familiarity with other technological matters. He also understood printing processes. Architectural construction and home decor also appear in works such as "Metzengerstein," "The Raven," "The Murders in the Rue Morgue," "The Purloined Letter," "The Fall of the House of Usher," "The Duc de L'Omelette," "The Pit and the Pendulum," "The Philosophy of Furniture" and "The Black Cat." Ballistics are used to identify the murderer in ".Thou Art the Man."

## The psychological context

We will never trace all of the sources for Poe's knowledge of psychology. His uses of such inspirations are, however, the more important consideration for us. Part of the Romantic impulse that swept western culture from the late eighteenth century into the nineteenth was a fascination with the human mind. After centuries of life during which scant study of the mind occurred, there was a significant change in outlook. Among American writers, William Cullen Bryant, in the early years of the nineteenth century, followed and surpassed by Ralph Waldo Emerson in particular, heralded the vastness of the mind itself, without the restrictions of older views of a God who was stern and, perhaps, narrow toward humans.

To Emerson, and to those who reacted, positively or negatively, to his works, the mind was akin to an uncharted territory, one which cried out for exploration. For such persons, the transcendental experience meant yielding to one's instinctive feelings, not literally rising off the earth, though his detractors often joked about levitation. Foremost in Emerson's conception of the human mind was that exploration would reveal essentially positive qualities residing there. He chose to express his ideas by means of lectures which, revised, were published in essay form. His typical unit of thought was the sentence, which listeners and readers sometimes could follow only with difficulty, though he did his audience the implicit favor of assuming that they could follow/comprehend his thinking. Emerson emphasized the value of individualism, though, paradoxically, his renowned essay "Self-Reliance" (1841) in fact encompasses individuality and outreach to others ("reliance" has the root meaning "rally," "connect"). In other words self-realization is not selfish, but connects the individual with others so as not to isolate one's self, creating balance/harmony in life. Many readers seem not to move beyond the idea that Emerson advocated staunch individuality of a sort that, were it carried to extremes, would produce anarchy. Poe was as eager as Emerson to explore the mind. In contrast to Emerson's optimism, Poe's outlook was less positive. For him the mind was a far more shadowy area, occasionally illuminated by unpleasant lights. The corridors of the mind reveal twisted pathways, which may provide surprises to the explorer, but those surprises are often the frightening discoveries that negative passions inhabit these environs. Yearnings for outreach leading to harmonious relationships with another or others are often hampered by reluctances to engage such bondings, be those reluctances mild or be they egotistical, brutal, murderous in nature. Poe's mistrust of mob rule may also have encouraged such skepticism, just as his shock at John Allan's refusal to provide him with financial security may have caused him to be skeptical even of individuals who seemed to be friendly.

Poe's creative writings are consequently peopled by characters whose emotions are fragile. He went far beyond the overwrought characters in antecedent Gothic fiction when he employed similar types, but for more creditable psychological purposes than are often found in those earlier works. His concept would have been that much in one's emotional life becomes fragile from inward causes that may be as dreadful as any that external sources arouse. Poe undeniably created terror that was rooted in the soul, employing strategies adapted from the Gothic tradition to convey that terror. Thus his writings continue to attract new generations of readers while those by others who were far more popular in his day are long forgotten, buried, and not prematurely, because they lacked the dynamic found in Poe's poems and fiction.

## The existentialist-modernist context

In Poe's early poem "The Lake," we encounter a speaker who with little modification might perform to similar advantage in many other literary works from Poe's day to our own. Poe's speaker is bereft because of some shattering emotional experience, such that he seems to enjoy the imprisoning confines of the lake and the trees surrounding it. This dark circle may be so physically restrictive (though the restrictiveness may be only imagined by the speaker) as to send the speaker's emotions spinning into fantasy. He, and we readers, have no inkling, as the poem concludes, of an exact cause for his fascination with death. He, and we readers, cannot foretell the future. The speaker is left in a meaningless void, thus positioning him as head of a long line of protagonists in American literary works. Poe later intensified what we might term the moral of this story. "Silence – A Fable" gives us an even more bleak portrait of a man undergoing a profane baptismal rite administered by a demon. The emotional turmoil in this ritual of demonic baptism conjures a vision of a geographical wasteland and desolation for the man on the rock. The structuring of the tale as a word-picture is intensified by the verbal repetitions, which produce a hypnotic effect, making the man who is listening to the demon's tale receptive to its content. His vision is, however, a bleak mirroring of his own condition. Both he and the man on the rock could be recreated in one of Gahan Wilson's horrifying graphics, with some creature lurking to devour the man (that rock is small), just as the listener's mind is being overcome by demonic power.

This technique provides one more example of Poe's turning to Gothic tradition, in which the persecuted protagonist opens the way for such persecution, though perhaps not realizing the nature of his/her receptiveness until tragedy occurs. Providing an entryway for non-rational force(s) is a common folklore theme (Poe repeats the theme in "The Raven"), and so the listener's giving admittance to a power he cannot control unleashes terrifying consequences. The protagonist and we readers are left without certainties as the tale concludes, and the multiple narrative framework serves only to blur further any anticipated clarification. The listener is left without any moral solidity, and such fragmentation is the essence in existentialist and modernist outlooks. The repetitive cadences and panoramic vision in "Silence – A Fable" recall, but ironically invert, much in the King James Bible. Although Poe was using a rhetoric and a situation familiar to his readers (whose knowledge of the Bible he could assume), the triumph of the evil or negative (or what I prefer to call the non-rational) being/force would have been a decidedly unexpected modification.

Two more examples will suffice to place Poe with the existentialist-modernist outlook: the destinies of the narrator in "The Fall of the House of Usher" and the dwarf couple in "Hop-Frog." Although Hop-Frog and Tripetta elude the powers of their oppressors, the King and his ministers, their own destinies are by no means clear-cut, thus resembling that of the narrator in "Usher," who escapes the collapse of the mansion and its inhabitants, but to what end we are not informed. With most of Poe's other protagonists we gain not even that much background. The majority remain nameless and they eventually lose their volition. Such open-endedness as Poe creates finds many progeny in literature, and in other arts as they march toward the present.

# Works

Poe's canon contains some of the most widely known literary works in the world. His early desire to be a poet has been gratified many times over, if from no other source than the popularity of "The Raven," one of the best-known poems in the English language, though many more reasons for such reputation exist. The early "To Helen ('Helen, thy beauty is to me . . .')," "The Sleeper," "The City in the Sea," "The Coliseum," "Sonnet – To Science," "The Bells," "Annabel Lee," "Ulalume" and "Eldorado": all are well known. Poe's critical dicta are likewise familiar and repeatedly cited, e.g. that a "long poem" is a contradiction in terms, that poetry must have a distinctive "music," that prose inclines more toward truth than poetry (beauty is the aim of poetry), that the brief prose tale is the greatest form in fiction, that the ideal reading time spans no more than an hour and a half. Poe's tales have, however, become his most significant legacy. "Ligeia," "The Black Cat," "The Tell-Tale Heart," "William Wilson," "The Fall of the House of Usher," "The Murders in the Rue Morgue," "The Masque of the Red Death," "MS. Found in a Bottle," "The Gold-Bug," "The Purloined Letter," "The Cask of Amontillado" remain favorites among makers of books, whether Poe's works themselves furnish the contents or whether one or another of these tales (or poems or critiques or *The Narrative of Arthur Gordon Pym* or *Eureka*, entire or excerpted) appears in selective compilations. Poe's tales and poems have often been targeted by parodists, though the emphatic rhymes and rhythms in the poems seem to invite more parodies than the fiction, from Poe's own day to the present, witness just one example: a recent roto-rooter promotional uses the catchy stanzaic and rhyme patterns from "The Raven."

The preceding roll call should not be read as if it includes the only works by Poe worth reading because they comprise his only genuinely artistic creations; far from it. For many years now, other tales such as "The Man of the Crowd," "Hop-Frog," "The Assignation," "Metzengerstein," "A Descent into the Maelström," "Morella," "Berenice," "Eleonora," "The System of Dr. Tarr and Professor Fether," "King Pest," "The Facts in the Case of M. Valdemar," to name several, have gained greater attention and admiration. Poe's novel *The Narrative of Arthur Gordon Pym* has likewise emerged from long years of neglect, winning commendation from Poe scholars and from many others.

Especially, though by no means exclusively, when considering the tales we must keep in mind that Poe was a journalist – who depended on the popular market for his livelihood, and produced fiction chiefly for financial returns – and not a systematic philosopher. Such heterogeneity places Poe firmly within the Romanticism of early nineteenth-century America (more about which below). Attempts to categorize his writings under particularizing headings, as anthologists tend to do, creates needless confusion, especially for those who are not familiar with the entire Poe canon. For example, "The Murders in the Rue Morgue" may be read as a detective story, as a Gothic thriller, as a text with contexts of sexuality and the violence frequently linked with it, or as a coded treatise, cast as fiction, of racial issues in Poe's day. "The Raven" admits of interpretations as a poem of the supernatural, yet many of the same passages used to bolster that reading yield equally valid evidence that here is a plausible, non-supernatural rendering of the protagonist's disintegrating mind. And how would the essay on street paving link philosophically with "To Helen" or *Eureka*?

Equally noticeable, *The Narrative of Arthur Gordon Pym* has since the 1950s become a veritable playground for critics, whose interpretations run a gamut from dismissals as dreariest trash (because Poe had no ability to compose a sustained book-length work, so runs this line of thought), through the suggestions that the numerous inconsistencies in the book make it a literary hoax, or that it is white Americans' paranoia, rendered as fiction, concerning African-American slave uprisings in the South, to its presenting a *Bildungsroman* depicting Pym's maturation. *Eureka*, Poe's last book, has been admired by some as interesting scientific thought, perhaps anticipating that of Einstein, and by others as yet another of Poe's spoofs. The subtitle, *A Prose Poem*, has unsettled opinions about classification even more. Each of these works (and assuredly many more by Poe) admits of being read within any of those contexts just named, as well as contributing to other approaches.

Whatever the precise circumstances, Poe's writings from first to last contain unmistakable evidence that attests Poe's awareness of much that we might call the essence of Romanticism in his time. American Romanticism relates to American life in general during the early nineteenth century. A major, if not *the* major, aspect of the Romantic outlook was a fascination with the human mind. Earlier western world outlook had considered the mind either a closed book or else a center of what ideally would be extreme rational intelligence. Thus arose a notion that norms existed against which all humans could be judged or to which all humans were supposed to conform. A key concept in Romanticism was, however, a curiosity about the mind/self, a curiosity that defied the limitations in earlier thought. Such curiosity assumed that the mind had in fact no closed doors, and that vast depths invited exploration. In America Ralph Waldo Emerson came to wield great influence, and the core of Emerson's thought was that the subjective or emotional part of mind was a center of positive force, which idea dovetailed with much in the contemporary American experience.

During this era strong individualism was often promoted as an essential to living everyday life. The nation was still new, so its maturing process or being on the move, so to call it, brought about discoveries of confrontations with much that was relatively unknown. What may have seemed to be an unlimited number of discoveries yet to be made in moving across the land fostered an understandable desire to have what was discovered be beneficial. Investigating what was still new territory bore resemblances to exploring the human mind. In his essay "The Poet," Emerson stated that America itself was a great poem. Since poems do not function explicitly in wholly rational planes, the mind seemed to contain much that was subjective. Emerson and those who subscribed to his ideas thought that exploring the human mind/self would reveal overwhelmingly positive discoveries. Emerson's concept of self-reliance was based on a mating of individualism ("self") with outreach ("reliance," which means "rally" or "connect"). Skeptics argued that while exploration of the mind/self was necessary and exciting, the discoveries might be grim. Journeying into the human mind/self might in fact reveal twisted and shadowy corridors instead of those brilliantly illuminated spacious areas, as characteristic of the self, the predominant concern in many important American texts, and therefore Emerson's reiterated motifs of light (usually the natural light associated with sun, moon, stars because the technology of lighting that we take for granted today did not then exist) and flowing water were refashioned into harsh, glaring illumination or overcast with vast darkness or as weird, terrifying lakes and seas. All were ambiguous, hence unsettling.

Poe's poems and fiction, which typically evince these latter qualities, are rife with decaying buildings and dreary landscapes (and seascapes), winding corridors that appear to be labyrinthine, spiral staircases (and other spiral motifs), weird tapestries, paintings and statuary, and shadowy or wholly dark areas either inside buildings or outdoors, both areas being representative of the mind/self. Inhabitants in these unpleasant places are equally gloomy. Settings in Poe's works often symbolize the human head/mind/self, and the relevant characters who reside within or those who confront terrifying externals (whirlpools or stagnant waters, dead trees and plants, bleak skies, storms) are as weird as their surroundings. Many Poe characters undertake journeys that present venturings into the mind, where disorientation often flourishes and overpowers. The explorations are unnerving, causing apathy in some, violent emotions (and actions) in others. The protagonists' claustrophobia is central in many of Poe's tales and poems, indicative of a gradual turning inward; the interior scene disturbs this protagonist even more than he was at the beginning of a given poem or tale. What emerges is a negative outlook on self-reliance; instead of a positive and unifying outcome, Poe's protagonists often experience isolation, anxieties and terror.

Poe was intent on demonstrating that the protagonist's terrors originate in and emanate from the mind, the "soul," to use his term in the "Preface" to *Tales of the Grotesque and Arabesque* (1840 [1839]). He contended that those who perceived only "German" (i.e. facile Gothic) substance in his tales overlooked his subtle modifications of terrors to function as credible psychological states (in all but a few of the tales). Where Poe learned about the nature of the mind/self is immaterial. The uses to which he put such education are his major artistic achievement. Many of his creative writings operate as dream structures, a fitting technique in psychological literature. A work opens with what appears to be credibility on the speaker-narrator's part, then shifts into increasingly dreamlike or fantastic planes. The lyric poem and the short story are perfect frames for such mindsets, and, as a dream may end, many of Poe's works lead us to an explosive conclusion. In effect, the protagonist awakens, or perhaps dies – dying an actual death or entering death-in-life, for example madness – providing closure as well for readers.

Vital, too, for attaining a good understanding of Poe's achievements is, or should be, an awareness and comprehension of revisions in his poems and tales and his attention to proofreading and other editorial principles. Poe was never satisfied with any version of most of his poems and tales, and so he made meticulous changes to them. A murky area in Poe studies often results, because, typically, readers of generations later than Poe's own usually encounter the last revised version of one of his works.

For certain writings, the latest version differs markedly from the text of the first publication, for example in the poem originally entitled "Irenë" but better known to us in its revised form as "The Sleeper," or in the poem "Lenore," where the commonly found form has longer lines than we encounter in the original form. Likewise as regards "Siope – A Fable" (better known by its revised title, "Silence – A Fable"), for which tale a manuscript version does exist, along with variant published versions. Comparisons of Poe's revisions illuminate his imagination at work. His changes tend toward improving a given piece and, usually, creating greater psychological plausibility. In the original *Burton's Gentleman's Magazine* version of "The Fall of the House of Usher" (1839) Poe cast Roderick and Madeline as identical twins. Since identical twins cannot actually be of different genders, Poe thoughtfully revised to make the brother and sister almost identical, thus achieving more accurate medical knowledge in this tale. A similar technique for creating precision may be seen in his altering the first title, "The Mask of the Red Death. A Fantasy" (1842), to "The Masque of the Red Death," which latter title imparts a greater sense of drama to that famous tale. Eliminating the opening paragraph in "Life in Death" ("The Oval Portrait" [1842]), wherein the narrator mentions that he was under the influence of opium, intensifies the idea that the human mind needs no assistance from externals to register awe and terror.[1] In general, the revisions in any piece intensify psychological realism.

We should also not ignore naming and diction in Poe's imaginative writings. For the most part, the speaker in a poem and the narrator in a tale are left nameless, perhaps to alert readers that these characters and their circumstances have universal appeal. When Poe does name his characters, those names tend to serve either a very serious or a decidedly comic purpose. Like many other writers, Poe was keenly aware of significant underlying implications in names, so he sometimes used place names that extend beyond face value. As with so much else in the Poe canon, names are subject to varying interpretations, which in turn allow many of the writings to suggest that any fixed meaning is questionable, perhaps because there is no single meaning within a particular poem or tale, and, moving farther afield, that life itself often does not consist in fixity. Such techniques align Poe with many of his contemporaries; for example, one need only consult critiques of *The Scarlet Letter* or *Moby-Dick* for parallels with critiques, say, of "Usher," "Ligeia" or *Pym*.

Poe was not unique in his careful diction. For comparison's sake, let us turn briefly to techniques used by a trio of relevant writers from his contemporaries. Emerson's repeated term *genius* inevitably is used in its root meanings of *creator*, more specifically *begetter*. The latter term usually implies *fathering*, or the (presumed) creation of vital new life/lives that in turn presumably will create additional lives. Most of Emerson's essays convey what we might designate a dramatic, indeed "charged," impact. In Hawthorne's "Young Goodman Brown" (1835), a story fraught with symbolism, most notably in the names of the protagonist and his wife, Brown is indeed young in worldly and philosophical experience. He is, however, curious about such experience, as represented by his attempt to step aside, if just once, and that briefly, from his Faith (his wife and the religious-philosophical planes of life she represents). "Goodman" may be the seventeenth-century equivalent of "Mr.," and so, along with "Brown" – one of the most widespread English names (then and today), used, perhaps, to impute universality to Brown and his experiences – ironic undercurrents may also be detected. With few alterations, "Young Goodman Brown" might figure as documents/testimony in many divorce court proceedings today. Melville's naming two principal characters in *Moby-Dick* (1851) Ishmael and Ahab might create shock value because those are not biblical names typically bestowed on male children.

## Poetry

Poe's output of verse is small compared with that of his fiction and critical writing, and compared with the far greater quantities of verse published by poets such as Milton, Tennyson, Whitman, Dickinson, Robinson or Frost, an irony because Poe wished to be recognized chiefly as a poet. Moreover, his poems, for the most part, contain such emphatic stanzaic patterns and rhymes that to some they do not seem to be serious art. Much more than mere sound (and no sense) informs Poe's poetry, as careful reading reveals. Although Ralph Waldo Emerson once spoke dismissively of Poe as the "jingle man," his remark was made after the very different verse of Walt Whitman had appeared, so the elderly Emerson may no longer have cared for the pronounced rhymes and rhythms typical in Poe's verse. Sound is crucial in Poe's poems, but sound does not subsume psychological plausibility; instead the sound promotes our apprehension of the sense, and that coalescence produces the success of the individual poem. Most of Poe's poems reveal emphatic rhyme schemes, but he could also achieve effective art in blank verse, especially in "The Coliseum" (1833) – although subtle rhymings enhance that poem.

Another fact worth remembering: Poe is not the protagonist in most of his poems (or in his tales). Instead his imaginative writings reveal very little influence from his personal circumstances, despite what much long-lasting mythology would suggest to the contrary. Assumptions that Poe is identical with the protagonist in nearly every creative work he published commenced in his own lifetime, and such notions continue strongly attractive for many present-day aficionados. Poe's poetry and fiction may convey considerable subjectivity, but that subjectivity emanates from the speaker within the poem rather than serving as a barometer to Poe's personal feelings. He was very much caught up in the contemporary culture of Romanticism. The principal mode of written expression in Romanticism was the lyric poem, and therefore the subjective emotions found in Poe's poems were not some aberration of a crackpot author written into his poetry, but those of his exquisitely, and consciously, wrought speakers.

Poe's poems display repeated themes and situations. First, his protagonist-speakers are males, who are usually emotionally disturbed, chiefly from the loss of a beloved woman. At times the protagonists are journeying, not so much over actual physical geographical terrain as in geography of the imagination, symbolized by means of landscape or other tangible details in setting. The speaker's overwrought mind makes him (they are all male) unreliable about his own state and correspondingly about what he perceives as he attempts to convey actualities in his circumstances. Notable exceptions are the more optimistic speakers in "To Helen" (1831), the second poem with that title (1848), "For Annie" (1849) and "Eldorado" (1849), as well as some of Poe's other poems addressed to individual ladies (and fairly negligible as poetic art).

In poems (and in some of the tales) involving less pleasant conditions, the speaker often seems intent on establishing or commanding power. A similar outlook occurs in most of the fiction, to be sure, and these likenesses are sometimes cited as limitations in Poe's creative abilities. Although decided likenesses exist among his characters and their circumstances, firstly Poe was writing in the trends of his literary milieu, where such protagonists were commonplace, and secondly, despite whatever similarities may be cited, sufficient variances prevent tedium. Just so, a vast readership admire Jane Austen's novels, albeit she confessed to polishing a small bit of ivory, thus expressing metaphorically her reason for working in what some might deem limited or confining materials. His handling of sounds in the poems has also elicited checkered reception; negative opinion argues that his rhyme and rhythmical patterns are so blatant because they mask deficient intellectual content. That same charge was leveled at Poe's contemporary, Tennyson, and, some years later, at Swinburne by their detractors, although such outlook has long been superceded by recognition of firm intellectuality in these poets, Poe included.

Poe's hope to win renown as a poet was natural for one with literary aspirations in the western world when he came of age during the 1820s. American writers at the time frequently emulated ancient Classical authors as role models, a natural since Greek and Latin had been signal components in European and American education for centuries. Another strong force upon authorship in this still fairly new nation was, understandably, British literature, though

French and German writings also had many admirers on this side of the Atlantic. In several respects, Great Britain continued to be regarded during the first half of the nineteenth century as the Motherland for Americans, attested by English predominating as the national language, despite large numbers of other European immigrants plus many African-Americans entering the new nation.

Divided attitudes toward just what literature should or might be (and what it should not) were evident. An emphatic strain of Neoclassical thought, which had been strong during the previous century, continued to influence much American literary endeavor, though a countering outlook resulted from the Romanticism that swept western culture as the eighteenth turned into the nineteenth century. Poe's writings emanate from both sources. Poetry retained high eminence in literary circles, though fiction was attracting expanding audiences. Drama in America tended to lag behind these other genres because the nation had no urban centers as customarily support theater activities. There were American play producers and playwrights, to be sure, and Poe himself once commenced writing a poetic drama. Nevertheless, the times still favored performances from British and Continental dramatists, and that tendency persisted well through the nineteenth century.

Poe has long been credited with an acute awareness of Romantic trends that emanated principally from British sources, although his education also keenly attuned him to the Greek and Latin languages and writings. Moreover, he had good command of French, but seemingly far less of German, though some German works came to him via translations. Since the Romantic impulse in Great Britain tended to poetic expression, whether in verse or prose, Poe naturally gravitated toward such forms. Much Romantic writing centered in landscape because of a renewed awareness of and interest in Nature, especially in its untamed state. Often, natural phenomena symbolized states in the human mind. A second important feature in Romantic writing was that of the introspective character, who appeared repeatedly in contemporaneous literature. Staunchly individualistic, despite circumstances that strongly militated against the wisdom of maintaining such a stance, the Romantic loner-hero became a major presence in the literature of the era.

Different though they were in many other respects, Wordsworth, representing the first generation of British Romantics, and Byron (perhaps to a lesser degree Shelley), for the second generation of Romantic poets, shared impulses to portray such subjective characters, though Wordsworth's generally gained some measure of emotional stability because they benefited from Nature's healing powers, while characters and themes in the verse of the other two just as often came to grief because of their individualistic choices and conduct.

Poe's own endeavors as a poet commenced with several works that betrayed strong leanings toward the poems of Shelley and Byron, whose influences are certainly distinguishable in Poe's first book (though they certainly did not end there), *Tamerlane and Other Poems* (1827).

Most of this brief volume is occupied by the title poem, a lengthy narrative in which the protagonist, modeled upon the great Asian warlord whose career was one of absolute dictatorship and frightening means of crushing his opponents, makes his deathbed confession to a priest. Poe's characterization of Tamerlane, who narrates this story in verse, resembles that of the Byronic hero, with a tinge of William Beckford's Oriental-Gothic novel *Vathek*, in which those damned to Eblis (the underworld) have their hearts set on fire. Tamerlane is not wholly terrifying. He had sacrificed his own youthful mild nature and the beautiful Ada, with whom he fell passionately in love while they were young, for military and overlord enterprises. His ambition, like Macbeth's, brings him power, but also despair. Like Byron's notorious protagonists, too, and behind them Frankenstein and Goethe's Faust, over-reachers therefore loners all, Tamerlane is doomed to emotional isolation from other humans because of his ambition. That Poe's Tamerlane relates the signal events in his life as a deathbed confession to a (Roman Catholic) priest may seem anachronistic, but this Muslim warrior may have had interests in Christianity.[2] Thus Poe's character is not so historically unrealistic.

In part, the blighted love in "Tamerlane" may reflect the thwarted love affair of Poe and Sarah Elmira Royster in that he deserted her to attend the University of Virginia, perhaps too to prove himself a monarch in poetry, his absence thus allowing her father to intercept their letters and direct her to marry another. Either legendary character or real-life young man returns to find that his beloved is dead to him. Whatever the origins of the poem, Tamerlane stands first in a long line of Poe's protagonists, individuals who are survivors of one sort or another, who consequently are not emotionally balanced or physically hardy. The dying Tamerlane is disconsolate because he has been deprived of feminine companionship. Many Byronic heroes (more precisely, hero-villains) sustain like emotions, and Poe's protagonists are subtle recastings of the Byronic character, though in characterizations Poe devotes greater attention to gender issues.

Other poems from the *Tamerlane* volume, "Fugitive Pieces" as Poe designated them, may be more accessible than "Tamerlane" itself. Poe's poems are visionary in overall appeal, and in many vision is enhanced by appropriate, hypnotic sound effects. Not for nothing do several of Poe's poems bear titles with the word "dream" being the operative term, and the majority of his poems may be reasonably likened to dream structures. A Poe poem begins, typically, in some mundane situation, then moves the speaker and readers into less rational planes. There we behold visionary scenes which, combined with the insistent, if monotonous, "music," draw us, just as dreaming does, away from everyday life into a fantastic world, a geography of the imagination rather than a mundane landscape. Thus Poe's poems are consistent with his notion of poetry and the poet. Poe's capsule definition, that poetry is "the rhythmical creation of beauty," dovetails with his repeated statements concerning "music" as an integral feature in poetry. We must remember that from time immemorial a poem has been equated with song and the poet with singer. Therefore Poe's poem-songs work, literally and figuratively, to enchant, i.e. to sing (persuade) readers into the world in a given poem. In other words, the poet as singer or musician uses his music to lure readers into accepting the poem on its own terms.

What better example of this technique than "To —," later entitled "Song." This poem tersely recounts the emotions of the speaker, an onlooker at the wedding of his former beloved, the sight of whom rekindles his passion for her, producing a daydreaming that takes shape as an interesting series of diffuse, somewhat shifting images which, however, always relate to fire, whether the flames are metaphors for his passionate emotions or for the blushes on the bride's cheeks, outward signs of her own emotions. Significantly, in context, diction of fire and desire relates to physical warmth, perfect minglings when passionate or blighted love is central. Perhaps the lady detects her former lover's presence and blushes in consequence, thus playing to his ego, which is wounded by her marrying another, yet self-congratulatory in that he supposes himself to be a better lover than her newly wedded spouse. The cliché blushing bride is, of course, subjected to the watcher's interpretations; thus her blushes, which may result from other causes, are in his mind assuredly connected with her embarrassment at his presence.

As in "Tamerlane," we find here a speaker who is emotionally dislocated because he has been separated from a female who once played an important role in his life, and who still exerts an emotional power upon him. That this poem is a song implies a more intense lyrical quality than the original title suggested (or that might inhere in any poems where song is not immediately impressed upon a reader), and that lyricism is a perfect vehicle for overwrought emotions. The stanzaic pattern recalls that in old ballads, in which blighted love was a reiterated theme, and since there is no elaboration on what parted the lovers Poe's poem also incorporates the vagueness of the traditional ballad. In other words, there are reactions which never solidify into detailed pictorialism or explanations, but which continue to shift before an intelligible picture or vision can form within the onlooker's mind.

Although other poems in the *Tamerlane* volume embodied the dream vision and flashback techniques, some also with Byronic themes, for example "Dreams," "Spirits of the Dead" (there entitled "Visit of the Dead"), "Imitation," "Stanzas" ("In youth have I known one . . . ") or "A Dream," the most significant for Poe's poetic development is "The Lake." This poem might be considered an anticipation, if a negative anticipation, of works like Thoreau's *Walden* or Melville's *Moby-Dick* in that, as in those books, the narrator is drawn to water as the origin of life and creativity. Poe's speaker is more nearly related to Melville's Ishmael because both present us with ambiguities as their respective works conclude. Poe's character alternates between delight and terror when, recalling his own vain love situation, he finds the lake itself, closed in as it is, a fitting emblem for his emotions. As the lake is swathed in a "pall," literally a covering for a coffin, though here the darkness of night descended upon the black rocks and tall pines ("tall" resonating with "pall" and "all" in the next lines, as if the speaker imagines a universal menace to love), the speaker is enclosed physically, therefore his imagination riots in hallucinatory sensations that bracket tangible sight with emotional envisioning of what has led to his loneliness. He has apparently eschewed love, and with the departure of the harmony that love inspires he becomes morbid. Such overpowering emotion does not permit extended, rational expression, so this brief poem plausibly combines sense with sound. Perhaps the couplet form represents an attempt to give an ordered expression to irrational thought.

Poe's next book of verse, *Al Aaraaf, Tamerlane, and Minor Poems* (1829), published in Baltimore by Hatch and Dunning, and with Poe's name on the title page, opens with the lengthy title poem, which has produced mixed reactions from readers because it yields no clear meaning. "Al Aaraaf" is an experimental, often confusing, work, part epic in impulse, part poem about poetics, with foundations in the works of Milton and Thomas Moore, two of Poe's favorite poets, and George Sale's edition of the Koran (originally 1734), upon which Moore drew in his long Oriental poem *Lalla Rookh* (1817), which may be Poe's more immediate source. A prefatory sonnet, "To Science," will be assessed below because it has usually been published as a separate poem from Poe's time to the present. Al Aaraaf is "a medium between Heaven and Hell," where in Arabian lore those who enter that region "suffer no punishment, but yet do not attain that tranquil and even happiness which they suppose to be the characteristic of heavenly enjoyment," as Poe outlined the piece to Isaac Lea, of the Philadelphia publishing house Carey, Lea and Carey. to try to interest him in publishing the poem (*O* 18–19).

"Al Aaraaf" is experimental in another way. Like Poe's later novels *The Narrative of Arthur Gordon Pym* and *The Journal of Julius Rodman*, or his uncompleted play *Politian*, this poem may be an incomplete work or an attempt at the Romantic fragment, then a popular form, witness Byron's *Don Juan*, Coleridge's "Christabel" or Keats's "Hyperion." Poe told Isaac Lea that there would be four parts to "Al Aaraaf," but only three appear in any extant version. The major theme is the nature of poetry itself. That poetry should be musical is made fairly clear, not just in certain ideas expressed, but in the forms of interspersed lyrics within the larger poem. Named characters, e.g. Ligeia, Angelo (based on the great Italian artist Michelangelo Buonaroti, 1475–1564), are associated with the arts (Ligeia in particular with sound), and with what art presumably creates, beauty.[3]

In Poe's theoretical conception, beauty is more than mere physical attractiveness. Indeed it is connected with balance and symmetry, or, in musical terminology, harmony. Music in "Al Aaraaf" wafts heavenward as lovely odors emitted from Al Aaraaf itself, attesting Poe's early definition of poetry: "Music when combined with a pleasurable idea, is poetry; music without the idea is simply music." Later he offered an even more terse definition: "I would define, in brief, the Poetry of words as *The Rhythmical Creation of Beauty*" (Poe's italics).[4] In an embryonic state, this concept is among Poe's endeavors in "Al Aaraaf." Since his venturing at epic – a desire that stimulated many other American writers during the nineteenth century – proved to be abortive, his ill success with "Al Aaraaf" may have led to his repeated dictum that a long poem is simply a contradiction in terms. The length of "Al Aaraaf" would not permit a comprehending reading of the entire work within an hour and a half, Poe's later stated time span for ideal response/comprehension when one engages literary works, and such length would also diminish the lyrical intensity so important to his theory of poetry. In Poe's culture (and for centuries preceding), music would have been inherently associated with brevity. Many years would pass before musical instruments would be powered by electricity, thus extending the sustaining of notes for far longer spans than Poe could have known. Brevity was, and remains of course, inherent in vocal music, and for Poe this type of music was inextricably linked with poetry. Consequently his comment, in the "Letter to Mr. —" prefatory to his 1831 *Poems*, that Milton doubtless preferred "Comus" to either *Paradise Lost* or *Paradise Regained* is consistent with his reiterated denial that a long poem could exist.

Revised versions of "Tamerlane," "The Lake" and others – grouped as "Miscellaneous Poems" – plus several new pieces, expand the book's contents. Of these, "Fairyland" and "To the River —" are the most significant. The former features an ambiguity: is this a wholly serious poem or do comic elements intrude? Are the moons – which seem to partake of human features ("faces"), and one of which, descending and as if it was a tent, overspread everything in its path – to be regarded as actual planetary bodies, or was Poe tongue-in-cheek in fashioning this poem? The abundant feminine rhyme, a form often used in comic verse, may substantiate jocularity here, and the lyricism verges on extravagance. Of course if the speaker is affected by moon madness (lunacy), then the barrage of sound may deftly convey his disorientation. Just so, "To the River —" may indicate an art–life symbolism, though since the River Po, a play on Poe's name, may be the focus, this poem may also be not wholly serious in intent.[5] The rhyme scheme evokes the meandering flow of the river, which repeats in the hazy mirror effect upon the girl's eye as she gazes into its wave(s).

To address the "Sonnet – To Science" is to approach a several-sided creation indeed. A long-standing reading advises that this poem is Poe's denigration of scientific rationalism as an opponent of poetry. We might note here, however, that the word "poetry" derives from the Greek, meaning "creation" or "creativity," since "poet" means "creator." Therefore poetry, which may define any type of creative art, is similar to the creation of new life, which is certainly the sense one gains from Poe's remarks that poetry excites the soul. In context, sexual creativity and artistic creativity are very much alike in reproducing part of the creator within fresh, dynamic results or, so to speak, "life."

"Sonnet – To Science" is subtle in these respects; although there may be a lament concerning what today we would perceive as a conflict distancing Science from Humanities, theme and form in Poe's poem may present other implications. If "Al Aaraaf" has epic qualities because of its cosmic implications, this far shorter poem features a potential epic conflict between science and poetry, but undercuts the drama inherent in such oppositions. First, the speaker would have us believe that he is an accomplished poet, but his choosing what in clumsy hands, such as his own, may be an exceedingly restrictive form, the sonnet, to express epic ideas is a severe limitation. Not only is the stanzaic form itself confining in its brevity (unlike many other sonnets), the trope of the poet as songbird and the mythological allusions seem to come direct from eighteenth-century Neoclassicism, which most nineteenth-century poets staunchly opposed. There may also be a touch of sexism, as we would understand it today, in the speaker's deploring what a female presence has done. This female presence, Science, daughter of time, may represent a realism that is essential to any genuine creativity, sexual or artistic, and that the speaker, actually a poetaster, fails to comprehend. Elsewhere in Poe's canon the importance of time, which affects all life, is emphasized. Here, what the speaker interprets as barriers set up by Science may really be counters to his too easy dreaming. That is, not all scientific thought is so coldly rational as to negate imaginative art. Since "Sonnet – To Science" continues as a perennial anthology piece, we should not read it as Poe's hostility to science. He was actually well informed about scientific thought in his day, as many of his writings reveal.

During his time at West Point Poe worked on a third volume, *Poems* (1831), published in New York City by Elam Bliss. Several of his important shorter poems were included, along with revises of "Introduction" (entitled "Preface" in the *Al Aaraaf* volume, but best known as "Romance"), "Fairyland," "Tamerlane" and "Al Aaraaf." "Romance" is significant because while the poet champions inspiration from romance, or creative imagination, that imagination is tempered with greater realism than casual readers might suppose. In other words, to be effective, a creative work must be founded upon reality. Therefore Poe's revision aligns with ideas he expressed elsewhere, e.g. in "Sonnet – To Science" and in "Israfel," in the 1831 volume, where the earthly poet notes differences between his poetry and that of Israfel, given that there may be fewer ideal conditions on earth than in the angelic singer-poet's heaven. Israfel is mentioned in the Koran as an accomplished angel-singer-poet, so his music would naturally appeal to Poe's thoughts about the music in poetry.

More of these early poems seem to veer among Oriental, biblical and Classical themes, natural topics for reader appeal in Poe's day, especially, as concerns the Oriental, in "The Valley Nis" (later "The Valley of Unrest") and "The City in the Sea," which Mabbott terms companion pieces (*M* 1: 196). Among Poe's contemporaries "Orientalism" more often meant the Near or Middle East rather than the Far East, and biblical references to ruined sites, along with archeologists' revelations, often touched on Oriental and Classical subjects. Both poems may be contextualized in the Gothic-Romantic outlook that ruins symbolized the temporality of human nature and aspiration. Structures that once represented strong, viable endeavors, e.g. Classical architecture and art (principally statuary) or, in more northern regions, the imposing Gothic cathedrals and the architecture in related religious centers, were in ruins by the nineteenth century. These ruins constituted excellent tropes for cultures' tangible and emotional shifts. The overall sound effects in both poems are pleasant, though the couplet form in both may register an attempt to give order to the chaos of ruins.

Companion reading may be found in "The Coliseum," which Poe submitted for the poetry prize sponsored by the Baltimore *Saturday Visiter* in 1833. The form in this poem differs from that in the other two. The speaker's "voice" is actually a meditation on the Coliseum's dwindling from an imposing center of teeming life into a ruined monument, which nonetheless may momentarily inspire awe in the beholder, who then, in a second thought, queries if all that remains is indeed the vestige of onetime greatness. The monument responds that no matter its physical decay, it still has sufficient power to call up memories of a glorious past. Poe's technique here might be thought to anticipate that of Walt Whitman, although Poe does not venture into free verse, but the blank verse in this poem is kept from prosaicness by means of the many rhymes that begin rather than end the lines. Blank verse is an excellent form for "The Coliseum" because the conversational or dialogue element in the poem reminds us that in his plays Shakespeare used blank verse as the chief form in a character's speech, which typically concluded in several rhyming lines.

Less pleasant but highly symbolic architecture and landscape enhance variously "The Haunted Palace," "The Conqueror Worm" and "Dream-Land," the last two composed a decade later than "The Coliseum." "The Haunted Palace" and "The Conqueror Worm" present us mainly with architecture, though the palace in the first poem is set in a fertile valley. The once lovely and sane but now unbalanced and terrifying "palace" symbolizes a mind. The "music" in the poem is appropriately intense because the theme in this song is mental disintegration. "The Conqueror Worm" offers a similar delineation of mental collapse, using a stage-play scene of a "house" (or mind) haunted by spectres of disease and madness that have led to literal or figurative death. This poem offers literary Gothicism with a vengeance, emphasized by a lurid "lights-out" conclusion that mimes techniques of theater performance. In "Dream-Land" Poe once again employs landscape imagery to symbolize a mind that has gone free-wheeling. The speaker's mind teems with woes, and so its recollections of a vast "world" in ceaseless upheaval bring satisfaction to the speaker because its mirroring emotional turmoil projects inner troubles onto a weird landscape peopled by equally weird inhabitants. The ghouls are threatening here, unlike those in "Ulalume," who are more sympathetic to the grief-stricken speaker. The insistent rhythmic patterns create a hypnotic effect that may literally enchant the speaker into the dream world of restlessness that he perversely enjoys.

Classical legendry provided background for what is possibly one of Poe's greatest poems, "To Helen." Helen of Troy was supposedly the most beautiful woman in the Classical world, though over time opinions about her have markedly differed.[6] For Poe, Helen's nurturing role not only literally brings the speaker (either Odysseus himself or a latter-day Odysseus figure) to a comforting home, but also stimulates his creative imagination, reminding him of the heritage of Classical art. The name "Helen" derives from Greek origins, meaning lightning, or dazzling light (compare "Electra"), which brilliant light makes impossible a sharp ocular focus on any physical allures, as is certainly the case in this poem. So Poe's Helen is idealized, and her ultimate statue-Psyche image, that of a winged illuminator for the speaker, offers multiple

perspectives. In Poe's creative works a male protagonist is inevitably depen-
dent on an integration with a female presence, else he cannot achieve his full
imaginative potential (and no doubt his physical-sexual potential, too, though
Poe's writing is anything but graphic in presenting sexual topics).

Brevity and pleasant rhythm coalesce with visionary tropes to create wholly
pleasurable reading. In popular parlance, the poem "flows" appealingly, with
no disruptions from rough, disjointed rhythms. The emotional trajectory leads
from the speaker's mention of the harmony emanating from Helen's beauty,
to his voyage on stormy seas, to his final rest at home, where her presence
continues to nurture and inspire him. The stanzas offer pictorial impressions
leading from panoramic ocean vistas to a felicitous picture-frame vision of
Helen as Psyche. This Chinese-box structure is great art. "To Helen" does not
devolve solely from biographical origins – that Helen represents Mrs. Jane Stith
Stanard, a beautiful lady who died young – or from Classical legend.[7]

Of neither Classical nor Oriental dimension, but a frequent anthology piece,
"The Sleeper" is another of Poe's misunderstood poems. Apparently some
readers find the entire poem too morbid, and one line in particular revelatory
of Poe's own (perhaps necrophiliac) inclinations. Taken out of context, line
48, "Soft may the worms around her creep!" may be repellant. If, however,
one reads the poem with some understanding of funeral customs in Poe's era,
which in part persist into the present, and with some understanding of a lover-
survivor's grief, the line and the poem may not be the least bit sensational.
Rather, both may exemplify creative writing firmly based in reality.

Readers are plunged into the puzzling opening episode of the speaker's
bewildered wandering at midnight under a moon that seems obscured by mist
that produces odd visual effects. The speaker's thoughts and vision subsequently shift to indoor scenes, then move slowly onward until he beholds the
corpse (of his beloved), prepared for burial, lying, as if asleep in the usual manner, on her bed. Only gradually does the survivor-speaker admit, and do we
realize, that the "sleeper" is actually dead. Next he envisions the procession to
graveyard and mausoleum. The tone in "The Sleeper" resembles the solemnity
and stillness appropriate to a funeral. The hushed orderliness is felicitously
expressed in the pervasive couplets, which are occasionally expanded into a
triplet to indicate that grief cannot be unceasingly contained.

"The Sleeper" depicts procedures related to viewing a corpse, then accom-
panying it to burial. In many funerals held in the deceased's home, as well as
those conducted in funeral parlors today, visitors do not directly, immediately
approach the dead. Moving instead from an entrance hall, perhaps turning at
an angle into the room where the corpse reposes, seems to be customary. In
funerals in the deceased's own home, the corpse is prepared on a bed, then

transferred to a coffin nearer the time when the funeral party prepares to move to the graveyard. Typically a solemn dignity is the intent. So the speaker's emotions gradually transform from denial, with his aimless wandering outdoors, to acceptance of his beloved's death, as sleep of the living becomes sleep in death. His vision of her in the tomb maintains concepts of pleasant sleep and unbroken silence, not to be disturbed by any discordant noise or images, and the line about the worms may plausibly be understood as his adjuring those creatures to preserve reverent silence while they move around, not through, the corpse.

So "The Sleeper" might be read more accurately as a work registering Poe's awareness of mundane events instead of a deliberate creation of sensationalism. Poe himself later credited the poem with greater artistry than that in "The Raven," his most famous work in verse. One might profitably read "Lenore," "The Raven," "Ulalume" and "Annabel Lee" as a cluster that is kindred to "The Sleeper." Like "The Sleeper," these later poems center in the death of a beautiful woman, a favorite theme with Poe, as I have already noted. Chronologically, "Lenore" was the earliest published of these pieces, and "A Paean," in the 1831 volume, may be read as a trial run for this poem. Poe's repeated revisions of "Lenore" indicate his high regard for the poem, though it lacks the rich suggestiveness found in some of the later poems. Unlike the survivor-lover in "The Sleeper," Guy de Vere, the speaker in "Lenore," is far more volatile in expressing his grief. Thus I concur with the verdict of Thomas Wentworth Higginson, expressed long ago (quoted in *M* 1: 330), that the first version of "Lenore" (with short lines) is superior to later versions with longer lines because I believe that Guy's intense emotional outpourings are more artistically wrought in the terse, choppy lines than in the longer, perhaps more eulogistic, lines in later versions.

"The Raven" has often been construed as a wholly supernatural poem, which, because of folklore that links ravens to the devil, offers one convincing approach to the poem. Equally convincing are the conditions that give credence to a non-supernatural interpretation, in which the speaker's delusions prompt him subjectively to incline *toward* supernatural underpinnings for his interaction with the raven. Poe plays upon the age-old gambit of a supernatural animal taking control of human victims, handling that theme in convincing fashion. The speaker's reading in those books of "forgotten lore," i.e. books of magic, may, in combination with the chanting effect in the rhythm of the poem, be all that is required to invoke an otherworldly presence, which takes the form of a raven. The bird is from a world outside the speaker's chamber (a chamber that may symbolize his mind/self), and, as is so typical in literary works in which supernaturalism operates forcibly, the non-rational world represented by the bird is not subject to human control. That the speaker has attempted to mitigate his grief by reading books of magic, which may contain spells appropriate for summoning supernatural creatures, is understandable. Like the survivor in "The Sleeper," this man cannot be held accountable for the means he chooses to assuage his sorrow, albeit his attempt produces unforeseen and uncontrollable consequences. Animal force triumphs over human reason, leaving the speaker motionless and speechless, as the repeated "still" makes clear.

Another convincing approach is that the speaker is utterly beset by grief, and that, as is suggested in many other creative works of Poe's, his is the loss of an ideal, symbolized in Lenore, who may have been no actual physical woman, but an emotional force that has nurtured the speaker's own emotional wellbeing. How he has managed to lose that part of what should be his fully integrated self is unclear, but in its absence he yields to notions of otherworldly influences, indicated, first, by his turning to books on magic and, second, by his attributing supernatural qualities to the raven, which in actuality it does not possess. Such a reading places "The Raven" as a solid psychological poem, in which the speaker manages to betray his own mental instability as the cause of terrors that lead to his ultimate loss of volition. This speaker appears to be only too ready to perceive his surroundings, which represent his own mindset, as those of Gothic horror. The midnight hour, his loneliness, the odd books he has been perusing until he becomes drowsy, the "ghost" on the floor, his bewilderment concerning origins of the rapping sound, his reluctance to open the door and window to his chamber (that is, to look outside himself?), and his reactions to the raven once he admits the bird: all hint of mystery and foreboding.

Mystery and foreboding dissipate (for readers), however, as we realize that in context "ghost" is nineteenth-century slang for the shadow cast by a fading ember onto a hearth, that any animal would seek shelter from the chill of a late December night (thus the raven was attracted to the speaker's quarters), and that, like any other wild bird, this one would enter but seek immediately for safety the most distant point from a human, here an art object on a high shelf, with the warmth of the burning lamp nearby. Granted, the single word the bird has been taught to articulate is unusual, but what is unusual does not equate with the supernatural. Instead the narrator imagines that the bird possesses traits that may have no bearing in actuality, even admitting more than once that his own "sad fancy," rather than supernaturalism, motivates his reactions. His fancy is assisted by the hypnotic effects in the incantatory rhythms and other sound effects throughout, to which he eventually so utterly succumbs that he becomes silent and immobile, signaled by the repeated "still" in the concluding lines. The repetition of "still" to suggest metaphoric death for the speaker reminds one of the equally subtle analogy of silence with death in "Sonnet – Silence" (1840). Moreover, as if to emphasize the disparity between sound and silence in the latter poem, Poe added an extra line, thus making his "Sonnet" a tour de force, which anticipates later experimentations with the sonnet form, for example by George Meredith in his sonnet sequence "Modern Love" (1862).

In this context, the speaker's own mind has departed from rationality because of the loss of Lenore, whose name – like Helen's, Eleonora's, or the other Lenore's in an earlier poem – hints of dazzling effects (she's "rare and radiant," and named by angels, that is, she represents an ideal) and great, if intangible, or, to use Poe's term, "supernal" beauty. Such qualities are difficult to preserve, and the speaker has evidently lost them. In other words, the light (of vitality, or creativity?) has departed from his life, ultimately plunging him into emotional darkness, represented by his sitting, silent and motionless, in the raven's shadow. Limited vocabulary, rhythm and rhymes may produce monotony, but the monotony betrays no limits upon Poe's imaginative abilities. Rather, it suggests that the speaker's fragile mind is manifest in the repetitions that may be symptomatic of emotional disorder. What remains, then, may be an exquisitely wrought psychological poem, which unfolds some extremely bleak circumstances. The speaker's condition at the end of the poem may very well seem analogous to symptoms evident in persons with Alzheimer's disease or senile dementia: the mind deteriorates and with that failing comes bodily degeneration. Therefore the speaker in "The Raven," composed so long ago, could be a very contemporary being.

"Ulalume" and "Annabel Lee," two late poems (respectively 1847 and 1849–50), likewise stand as excellent minglings of sound and sense to chronicle the death of a beloved lady. In "Ulalume," wandering with his companion, Psyche (representative of his own nurturing emotions), the speaker unheedingly draws near the tomb of Ulalume, whose death has rendered him irrational. As in "The Sleeper," where moon madness (lunacy) initially overwhelms the speaker, we encounter in "Ulalume" astrological lore concerning planetary causes for troubled love. The name of Ulalume, suggestive of moonlight, may also point to lunacy in the speaker. Events in the poem may plausibly occur on Hallowe'en, when temporary influence of supernatural powers may motivate the speaker's forlorn quest. As if he anticipated present-day customs of trick or treating, Poe so situates the speaker and Psyche that the eerie circumstances of the October night make the speaker ignore Psyche's cautioning him to turn from death-related circumstances. That their journey concludes at Ulalume's tomb brings death-in-life (what a perverse treat) to him; like many other Romantic characters, the speaker cannot cope with reality. As in Hawthorne's "Young Goodman Brown" or Henry James's *The Portrait of a Lady*, the protagonist's future remains uncertain, but probably gloomy, if indeed there is a future for the speaker in "Ulalume." Just as "The Raven" ends with a physically and emotionally benumbed speaker, so the later poem leaves the speaker unmanned, without the anticlimactic sense that some readers may feel as "The Raven" closes. The hypnotic aura in "Ulalume" meshes superbly with the speaker's incoherence in the face of his loss, which is reflected in speech that might be likened to rather aimless repetitious mutterings until he realizes that he has reached the tomb.

Sound and sense in "Annabel Lee" may be read as a counterpointing to the sonorous gloominess in "Ulalume." Annabel's survivor-lover's words are lilting in comparison with those spoken on the eerie October night. Although events connected to Annabel's death seem to be long past, her frustrated lover intensely remembers them. The light tone in the poem may in fact be an accurate means of conveying hysteria, which grips him whenever he recalls her death. As regards the lasting effects of bygone events, Annabel's lover resembles Fortunato in "The Cask of Amontillado" or – if we admit that a long time elapses between the sensationalism itself and the time it is related to us – the narrator in "Ligeia." Annabel's lover's words seem to mime the rising and falling tides in the sea as he alternates between fleeting happy memories of their love and the reality of his grief.

"Annabel Lee" is indeed a typical Victorian love poem because it enforces the custom of remaining true to just one lover. Like the speaker in "The Sleeper," Annabel's lover has some irrational thoughts about causes of Annabel's death, attributing her demise to machinations of supernatural beings who are jealous of such intense love as Annabel and he enjoyed. Such an idea is characteristic of a grief-stricken survivor's pondering the cause of a loved one's death. As in "The Sleeper," too, "Annabel Lee" does not run to any necrophilia on the speaker's – or Poe's – part as he imagines lying down by Annabel. Such imaginings are predictable fantasies of what circumstances might have been, had Annabel lived. There are no ghastly features of a corpse nor whiffs of decay in the speaker's fantasies. Instead the closing lines may be suggestive of awareness that he is approaching death (a plausible thought because so much time has elapsed since Annabel died). Thus the poem recalls a similar condition in "The Assignation," where the mutual suicide pact is predicated upon the lovers' rejoining each other in a union after death. Immortality is strongly hinted in both works.

Finally, the repetition of Annabel's name throughout the poem contributes another strong linking of sound with sense. The name literally means "beautiful

Anna," and Anna means "gracious" and "merciful." "Gracious" derives from "agreeable," which quality is evident in our information regarding the love of Annabel and the speaker. "Merciful" may also mean "loving," and that state, too, obtains in this poem. To paraphrase, the speaker has lost beauty, grace and love, all those qualities suggesting balance. No wonder, then, that the grief-stricken lover uses song to convey the intensity of his lament.

A group of poems for final consideration are far less gloomy than those surveyed above, thus affording us glimpses into what many might designate as Poe's less characteristic type of writing. For example, Poe apostrophized Frances S. Osgood, Sarah Helen Whitman, Mrs. Nancy Richmond and Marie Louise Shew in several platonic poems. The lingering illness from tuberculosis of his wife and her death in early 1847 left Poe bereft, and although he continued to live with and support Mrs. Clemm, his mother-in-law, he nonetheless cherished his warm friendships with women nearer his own age. In an age when platonic verse enjoyed widespread popularity, these poems are the natural expressions of one who valued such acquaintances. In this same vein, "To My Mother" reveals Poe's pleasure in the nurturing companionship of Mrs. Clemm.

Another cluster of poems that embody greater ambiguities are "To One in Paradise," "The Bells" and "Eldorado." The first, originally published as part of his tale "The Assignation" (then entitled "The Visionary"), unfolds an outpouring of emotion for a lost love, but whether the beloved lady has died or has been for reasons unexplained taken away from the speaker we cannot determine. The metaphors of light extinguished in the speaker's life because he lost his inamorata, and those of the stricken eagle and the blasted tree derive from Byron's poems, understandably because "To One in Paradise" is the creation of a Byronic poet. This poem may also be read as an anticipation of the equally intense frustration and grief of the speaker-singer in "Annabel Lee."

"The Bells," often dismissed as a mere welter of sounds, reveals in a more thoughtful reading a poem about life's passages from birth to death, each stage signaled by a different type of bell. The buildup from quietness to an increasing crescendo in each section of this poem suggests the alternation from lows to highs that characterizes the progression from birth to maturity, perhaps to marriage, and on to death. Such a theme makes "The Bells" kindred to "The Masque of the Red Death," in which a progression through life, sometimes designated "the seven ages of man," is set forth (*M* 1: 667–68, 677 n3). Finally, "Eldorado," another late poem, is structured as a realistic journey through life. As death approaches, the speaker, a knight questing for "Eldorado," learns that that fabled territory has no actual geographic location, but that it is instead a state of mind, and that to achieve that state of mind one must not give up questing, else life holds no zest. Like "The Coliseum," "Eldorado" is a dialogue poem, one that demonstrates Poe's certain touch in employing dialogue. The swift pace of this song suggests that life often passes rapidly before death is realistically faced, and the swift rhythm simultaneously hints that life should be alive and vital instead of mere passive passage through conscious existence.

A final poetic work for consideration is Poe's hastily written, uncompleted play, *Politian*. Composed during the mid-1830s when Poe was casting about to find a suitable medium that would pay, this dramatic fragment, intended for the stage, has never numbered among Poe's widely admired achievements. Based on an actual triangular love affair in the 1820s, customarily called the "Kentucky Tragedy," the play does not seem to offer much dramatic action. Poe published eleven scenes (others were lost) in the *Messenger*, and, reluctantly, in *The Raven and Other Poems* (1945). The revenge theme makes *Politian* companion reading to "The Cask of Amontillado" and "Hop-Frog," although that same theme bears some resemblance to what we find in "Berenice," "Ligeia" and "The Fall of the House of Usher." The narrators in these tales seem to bear less than wholly good will toward the female characters. The Italian element and threatened violence also bond *Politian* with "The Assignation."

## The fiction: tales

"Poe's tales are his chief contribution to the literature of the world." So begins Thomas Ollive Mabbott's "Introduction" to the "Tales and Sketches" volumes in *Collected Works of Edgar Allan Poe* (xv). This declaration, from the longtime doyen among Poe specialists, is not to be taken lightly. Although, as is well known, Poe's principal wish was to be a poet, he realized no financial returns from the three volumes of verse he published between 1827 and 1831. Consequently he turned for financial reasons to writing prose fiction, and although his sum total literary income proved to be meager, even if one compares inflation rates between his era and our own, Poe quickly learned how to write artistic brief tales, eventually turning out almost seventy, of varied characteristics and qualities, a spectrum ranging from ghastly horrors in "The Pit and the Pendulum" or "The Murders in the Rue Morgue" to light comedy in "Three Sundays in a Week," or from the serious, but not terrifying, landscape visions in "The Island of the Fay" and "The Domain of Arnheim" to the extravagantly satiric mode in "Loss of Breath." Poe wrote and published fiction in hopes of financial gain, and although he is best remembered as a writer of Gothic horror his stories are actually not of just one type but reveal greater variety, as might be expected from a journalist eager to write what would sell. Moreover, as I remarked previously, *The Narrative of Arthur Gordon Pym,* in certain respects an outgrowth from Poe's experiments with short fiction, has since the mid twentieth century elicited more, and more respectful, considerations of its art. A continuing problem in engaging Poe's fiction is that of uncertainties among readers, originating in his early aims and intents for his tales.

Significantly, popular fiction, so far as Poe was concerned, was, for the most part, the type that appeared in such prestigious literary periodicals as *Blackwood's Edinburgh Magazine,* established in 1817, and other British magazines of the day, for example *The New Monthly* and *Fraser's,* emulated by Americans eager to promote their literary credibility. What continued over many years as staple fiction in these publications was the terror tale, the scaled-down descendant of Gothic novels that had flourished from the 1790s on into the second decade of the nineteenth century, and that had a great impact on subsequent western world literary culture. Despite harsh criticism from critics, who were used to greater restraint in literature, Gothicism entered American literature during the 1790s, first in stage plays by William Dunlap, the so-called "Father of American Drama," next in several novels by his friend Charles Brockden Brown, thence from the pens of many other writers eager to draw upon popular models, which they adapted to the American scene. That Poe should go to work writing terror tales was thus unsurprising.

A second type of popular fiction, the comic mode, also strongly appealed to Poe. More important, many writers discerned how to mingle horror with humor within an individual tale, and so we may find many with initial hints that supernaturalism is besetting the protagonist, only to discover in the conclusion that the narrator had a nightmare or that his fantastic circumstances resulted from his drunken irrationality or the hallucinatory effects produced by drugs, opium being the most commonly ingested substance among these narrator-protagonists because it was easy to obtain for medical uses. Thus the con man became a popular literary character. Manipulations of terror-tale elements became a chief *modus operandi* for many writers from Poe's era on into the present day, and Poe was a prime mover in modifying literary Gothicism from what was intended to provide little other than lurid thrills for readers all too eager to receive them (no matter how improbable the circumstances in such tales), into a psychologically sophisticated literary art. Several of Poe's poems, most notably "The Raven," "Ulalume," "The Sleeper" and "The Conqueror Worm," manifest this tendency, but he published more fiction in which such achievements obtain.

The years (1831–33) when Poe turned to the writing of fiction remain just about the most obscure period in his life, but we may justifiably surmise that

3 2783 00113 7671

PRAIRIE STATE COLLEGE
LIBRARY

he undertook a study of Gothicism that resembles an academic independent study course on today's campuses. Poe studied the nature of and experimented with creating effective short fiction. Although it has become a commonplace to cite Poe's dictum that the short story is a sophisticated literary form because it admits of creating a unity of impression or effect, which tales can be read within an hour and a half, his critical pronouncement followed several years after his own publication of short stories had commenced. Between those beginnings and, say, his May 1842 review of Hawthorne's *Twice-Told Tales*, in *Graham's Magazine*, in which he formulated his theory about the short story, Poe had published some of his finest tales, e.g. "MS. Found in a Bottle," "The Assignation," "King Pest," "Silence – A Fable," "Shadow – A Parable," "Ligeia," "The Fall of the House of Usher," "William Wilson," "The Murders in the Rue Morgue" and "The Masque of the Red Death." He had collected the tales that originally circulated in periodicals into two volumes entitled *Tales of the Grotesque and Arabesque* (1840 [1839]).

A surprise awaits those who suppose that Poe invented the Gothic horror story and published fiction strictly in that vein. Not only did he not invent lurid sensational fiction, but when his tales began to appear during the 1830s many reviewers deplored what they saw as a promising young writer's waste of time and talent in publishing "German" (for which read "Gothic") fiction, which, of course, according to certain critical schools of thought, could not be first-rate literature. Within the same or in other notices of Poe's early tales – notices that were often reprinted for promotional purposes in the *Southern Literary Messenger*, and that have been reprinted in recent years, many of them in *The Poe Log* – are comments that may disconcert aficionados who imagine that these notices would naturally carry information about Poe's tales being thriller or ghost-story fiction. Instead such readers may encounter perceptions of a comic impulse underlying Poe's lurid tales. Therefore the long-held notion that Poe was deranged in his everyday life, and that his derangement, which may have originated in or stimulated immoral propensities (in his personal life and therefore transmuted into his writings), accounted for the weird tales he published, must diminish in the face of realities expressed in the literary marketplace of early nineteenth-century America.

A bit of literary history should clear away bewilderment over what Poe, long touted as a fine, maybe the finest, American creator of ghostly stories, may have composed in the comic vein. Evidence exists to reveal that he planned, and nurtured for several years, a book that, had it seen publication, might testify to his being one of America's great humorists instead of a purveyor of sensational writings, usually, but not exclusively, with supernatural underpinnings. That projected book, "Tales of the Folio Club," involved much effort on the part of aspirant fiction writer Poe, and that it did not appear results from an irony that we must attribute to Poe's wanting the best for his book. Thomas White, owner of the *Southern Literary Messenger*, was willing to bring out Poe's book, but Poe apparently desired a more prestigious publisher. Consequently he negotiated with several publishing houses in the northeast, none of which agreed to produce his book, and eventually the project collapsed. Then he published individual stories in literary annuals and magazines. Divorced from the framework of the book, these tales elicited mixed responses from readers, who were puzzled by the mixtures of comic and Gothic elements.

To move from matters of literary history to the contents in Poe's "Tales of the Folio Club," we find that he was basing his book in part on established models of frame narratives that extend from Classical literature into his own times, and that he was attempting in part to lampoon some widely popular authors (principally fiction writers) of his day. Had "Tales of the Folio Club" appeared as Poe planned, it would have featured monthly meetings of literary men, members of the Folio Club, who were pompous and pretentious about their status as creative writers and their literary acumen. Surviving Poe's eventual dismantling of his book are manuscript portions of a prologue – which lists terse descriptions of the club members and doubles as a table of contents for the book – and a version of "Silence – A Fable" (originally entitled "Siope – A Fable"). Poe's aim was to fashion each club member as a caricature of some best-selling writer, whose tale would satirize or parody the methods of its real-life model. Each presenter would also serve as first-person narrator within the tale resembling his own type of writing.

Every month the person whose tale was voted best at the previous meeting served as president. He whose tale was ranked worst acted as host, providing the meeting place and ample drink and food. Following each reading was a debate over its merits and demerits. Partaking of too much food and drink, the club members' minds would become muddled, and gluttony and intoxication often enhanced these early tales. In tandem with the overinflated self-esteem of most members, the food and drink added to tendencies for imperfect evaluations. Arguments about the tales, plus the tales themselves, would have heightened humor throughout the book. Eventually, the person whose tale was voted worst several times in succession took umbrage and fled with the manuscripts to a publisher to circulate an exposé of pretense and folly within the Folio Club.[8]

The tales vary in content. Poe specialists have argued that the first five published stories were parts of the Folio Club: "Metzengerstein," "A Tale of Jerusalem," "The Duc de L'Omelette," "Bon-Bon" (as "The Bargain Lost") and "Loss of Breath" (as "A Decided Loss"). The last four of these tales are fairly evident lampoons of writers such as Horace Smith, N. P. Willis and Benjamin Disraeli, along with the host of terror tales in *Blackwood's Edinburgh Magazine*. Poe submitted his five tales to a prize competition sponsored in 1831 for 1832 publication by the Philadelphia *Saturday Courier*, a weekly newspaper (newspapers in Poe's day featured more literary material than we are used to finding in today's newspapers). Although none of Poe's submissions won the prize, all were published anonymously during 1832. Just when Poe may have begun "Tales of the Folio Club" is uncertain, but he revised these tales – "Bon-Bon" and "Loss of Breath" extensively – before they reappeared in the *Southern Literary Messenger* several years later.

"Metzengerstein," first of the five to be published (14 January 1832), was subjected to four revisions, each diminishing any comic context as it evolved into a prose-poem of subtle psychological dimension. "Metzengerstein" is the first of several tales in the Poe canon that depict human nature shifting toward bestial behavior, a theme picked up again in *The Narrative of Arthur Gordon Pym*, "The Murders in the Rue Morgue," "The Black Cat," "The Raven" and "Hop-Frog." To enrich the theme of metempsychosis (transmigration of souls) in "Metzengerstein," Poe draws on folk belief of disastrous consequences for unions between humans and non-humans. This theme is evident in the bonding of Baron Metzengerstein with the giant horse (a reincarnation of the vengeful spirit of the Berlifitzings, with whom the Metzengersteins long continued a deadly feud). Similarly, "The Assignation" presents such an excellent blurring of human with statuary in the illicit amour of the stranger-hero and the Marchesa Aphrodite that we might overlook Poe's use of folklore regarding disastrous unions between human and non-human lovers, though Poe's treatment compares favorably with that in the Don Juan legend and others that treat human relationships with statues. Poe adapted other folk tales, for example modifying the Flying Dutchman legend in "MS. Found in a Bottle" and adapting comic folk motifs involving disguises used to play upon the misperceptions of others, for example "The Man That Was Used Up" or "The Spectacles."

To suggest how an individual work by Poe may satisfy various approaches, all of them equally valid, let us return briefly to the place of "Metzengerstein" in the Folio Club. There, the most likely teller, Mr. Horrible Dictu – who has Germanic associations that would dovetail with the "German" (Gothic) nature of the tale – would have presented the sixth reading. Therefore the seemingly straight "German" tale that "Metzengerstein" may be would doubtless draw commendation from the group, whose awareness had been dulled by too much alcohol and food. In a like vein, "MS. Found in a Bottle" makes alert readers (unlike the Club members) question the validity of the narrator's story, if they divine that a drunken Club member's fantasies may create the apparently overwhelming, and even supernatural, horrors that eventuate in the narrator's death. The tale commences plausibly enough, but once the presumed supernatural ship and sailors emerge we encounter some superb wordplay on alcohol, e.g. in "spirit" followed by mention of imbibing and "ruin," all in the sixth from final paragraph, which may signal the narrator's drunkenness. "Ruin," though it is more customarily "blue ruin," was contemporaneous slang for low-grade gin (reiterated in "King Pest," another tale that may have taken part in some version of "Tales of the Folio Club").

If we accept "MS. Found" as a drunkard's tale, at least for its quondam role in the Folio Club, then episodes that are too outrageously sensational to be credible are very understandable if they are the disorienting experiences of a a drunkard. If Mr. Solomon Seadrift read this tale to the Folio Club as one of his recognizable compositions, his own name offers a combination of wisdom (Solomon) and untrustworthiness (Seadrift). The motto to the first published version of the tale, "A Wet Sheet and a Flowing Sea," a line from the Scottish Allan Cunningham's verse, hints more tellingly the nature of this tale: unlike our own era's need for three sheets to the wind to signal intense drunkenness, just one sufficed in Poe's day. The flowing sea might be read as a forerunner to Mark Twain's *Adventures of Huckleberry Finn* (1885), wherein drunken Pap Finn's quantities of vomit inspire Huck's thought that taking sounds would constitute the only accurate means to measure the depth. "MS. Found" is, however, in part based on a scientific, or pseudo-scientific, concern much in the popular mind during Poe's time, the "holes at the poles" theory, to use the colloquial phrase for possible entrances at the north and south poles into the earth's center. Thus when the giant ship descends in a whirlpool at the end of Poe's tale, we are left to wonder whether that descent is scientifically credible or if it represents a drunkard's nightmare.

Similar multiplicity obtains in "The Assignation," originally entitled "The Visionary." What may appear in cursory reading as a bit of frothy melodrama involving illicit lovers' sexual pleasure also suggests a segment of Byron biography – the great British poet's affair with the Italian countess Guiccioli. The tale may also convey subtle implications about life–art intersections, and it is Poe's first treatment in prose of what he termed elsewhere the greatest poetic theme, the death of a beautiful woman. Read in this way, "The Assignation" functions as a hoax upon Byron and Byronism, both immensely popular subjects in Poe's literary milieu. Poe has fun in fictionalizing what his Byron's life should have been, the cream of the jest being that the narrator is a caricature of Byron's biographer, Thomas Moore, the Irish poet, who may be like the earlier British philosopher and statesman, Sir Thomas More, who supposedly jested on his way to execution. Moore also had the reputation of publishing salacious verse, so his presence in Poe's tale increases the multiple comic intentions found here.

That Thomas Moore, reputedly fond of drink and of publishing salacious verse, should be recreated as the Mr. Convolvulus Gondola who narrated "The Visionary" provides another comic touch to this tale. The narrator, like his heroic acquaintance, is a visionary, but his vision remains imperfect, firmly confined to "seeing" sensuality and tangibles, so he does not comprehend the nature of love in the same way the suicidal pair do. In another reading the tale yields a symbolic rendering of matters inherent in an integrated self. The weird art collector-athlete-hero cannot survive without a firm bonding with his beloved, or, in other words, masculine–feminine balance/harmony is essential for genuine life and integrated self, be that a life/self one of domestic happiness or one of artistic creativity. Artistic achievement may parallel new life as an outcome of sexual creativity, represented by the baby (and by the portrait of the Marchesa, which is lifelike), doubtless fathered by the dynamic stranger-hero rather than the Marchesa's old and apparently sterile husband, whose inactivity and feeble strumming of a guitar suggest an apathy that does not promote and is incapable of any type of creativity. Perhaps suicide, i.e. death of the self, is given a more positive implication here than is customary. To emphasize that shedding one's self-directed plans because of true love, in the sense of "charity," or giving to others, is uppermost in the tale. Finally, this tale includes art–life implications in the Marchesa–stranger–statuary linkages.

"Silence – A Fable" also invites multiple interpretations. The original title, "Siope – A Fable," furnishes in the first word a transliteration into English of the Greek word "silence." That same word suggests the anagram, "Is Poe," which in the Folio Club would match this tale with the "very little man in a black coat with very black eyes" among the club members. Granted, Poe had grey eyes, not black, but his black coat became an identifying hallmark of him for others. The setting and the pervasive anxiety place the tale with the scenic and emotional effects found in Poe's early poems of bleak landscape and psychological unrest. The language, which may be reminiscent of that in the King James Bible, could as readily be the babbling of a drunkard reading to the drunken Folio Club group.

Read as more serious art, distanced from the Folio Club framework, the language might just as plausibly be the repetitions of the narrator (left terrified, incoherent and stuttering from the vision shown him by the demon during a perverse baptismal rite), in trying to repeat the demon's words. The incantatory sound techniques may also hint of the gripping power of the demon as he increasingly dominates his victim, spellbinding him in several senses. The narrator's vision, conjured by the demon, of the man on the rock may represent his own looking into the demonic (non-rational) depths of his soul and the turmoil that vision creates in his emotions. As the tale concludes, the lynx, a creature associated with perfidy, can laugh, but the narrator's state of shock leaves him as a reminder to us of how like later existential thinkers Poe may have been. Extremely intense, the tale is brief, as if to remind us that strong emotion is of short duration. Whatever implications may inhere in "Silence – A Fable," that very title suggests that it invites varied interpretations (and the on-rushing language in the tale certainly suggests that silence is indeed a fable, i.e. no silence at all). Despite its weird features, "Silence – A Fable" is another of Poe's appeals to readers in his own day. Many could identify with the language, that of the Bible and the pulpit oratory that employed similar language structures. The situation in the tale seems much like the temptation of Christ by Satan. "Silence – A Fable" may in theme and form resemble other works from Poe's day, for example the humorous sketches "The Harp of a Thousand Strings" and "Where the Lion Roareth and the Wang-doodle Mourneth," attributed to William Penn Brannan.[9]

Among these early stories that possibly figure into some version of the Folio Club project, "Shadow – A Parable," "Lionizing" and "King Pest" stand out as encapsulations of the overall drift in Poe's book. The first, in language also reminiscent of the King James Bible, portrays mourners gathered around the coffin of their latest departed friend. They drink heavily, perhaps to stave off thoughts of death's inevitability, but they are finally terrified by the appearance of Shadow (of death) as the tale closes. The somber dignity of the group may be reminiscent of comic aspects of the presumably dignified and astute, but in reality pretentious and intoxicated, Folio Club members. "Lionizing" and "King Pest" may proceed in a more humorous direction that mimes the disruption within the Folio Club when their latest inductee, outraged at what he considers preposterous treatment of his writing by a group of self-congratulatory, second-rate writers, flees with the manuscripts to a publisher to expose the Club's pretentiousness. The amusing critical remarks by various characters in these two tales may likewise target the members' weak but pompous attempts at criticism. The plague motif in "King Pest" may well satirize the nature of the Folio Club enterprise (a plague on worthwhile authorship and criticism) in addition to whatever other purpose it serves within the tale proper. "Lionizing" and "King Pest" include sufficient material of a literary nature enfolded into the plot structure, where routs are highlight episodes, to reinforce possibilities that either piece, in one version or another of the Folio Club experiment, may have been the concluding tale, a mimicking in miniature of the Club's proceedings.

Failing to secure publication of the Folio Club book, Poe dismantled it and circulated individual tales in literary periodicals. He entered what was a portion of the manuscript for "Tales of the Folio Club" as a submission for the fiction prize offered by the Baltimore *Saturday Visiter*. Long afterward one of the judges revealed how he and the others were hard put to select one of the tales as best because all were fine. "MS. Found in a Bottle" probably came out the winner because it was nautical fiction when Baltimore was far more maritime than we think of it today. One of the judges, John Pendleton Kennedy, was so impressed by the high quality in these tales that he assisted Poe in securing employment and outlets for his writings. Consequently "MS. Found" reappeared in *The Gift for 1836*, and Kennedy urged Poe to send tales to other periodicals. That "The Assignation" ("The Visionary") appeared in *Godey's Lady's Book* (January 1834) indicates Poe's alacrity in heeding Kennedy's counsel. This thoughtful attention may have combined with Poe's own observations of what to publish where, because *Godey's* in these years regularly featured sensational fiction set in Italy. Years later *Godey's* published another Poe tale with partial Italian elements (*M* 2: 255–56), "The Cask of Amontillado" (1846).

After the Folio Club book failed, Poe must quickly have realized that he must really dispense with the externals of alcohol and any other intoxicant, much less gluttony, in creating characters who speak with the same incoherence and act from a bewilderment similar to what we encounter in the gluttons and alcoholics in the Folio Club or like the    drug addicts who often appeared in popular fiction of the day, and from whom Poe may have derived several of his characters, e.g. the narrators in "Ligeia" (1838) and in the original version of "The Oval Portrait" ("Life in Death" [1842]) or those who think about drug addiction, e.g. the narrator in "The Fall of the House of Usher" (1839). Poe would also continue to employ trappings and themes of antecedent Gothicism – decaying architecture or bleak landscapes and the stereotypical plot of vicious pursuit of innocence for purposes of lust, money or power, often related to family identity involving physically or emotionally debilitated characters, gender issues, sexuality, and perhaps, as some recent critics argue, even racial issues.

Sometimes we encounter genuine supernaturalism, for example in "Metzengerstein," sometimes what only seems to be supernatural, as in "The Premature Burial" (1844). Such themes Poe would craft to suit his own intents and techniques in composing what in "How To Write a Blackwood Article" (1838) are called tales of "sensations" or, in "The Murders in the Rue Morgue" (1841), "mystery [or] romance." Any of these terms, or "German," are synonyms for what has long been called "Gothic." The shifts away from literary and intoxicant motifs are apparent in many of Poe's later tales, and not just those that seem to be perennial favorites among anthologists. Whatever the particular features of Gothicism Poe may have employed in a given work, the development of disorder or the creation of a frisson is not necessarily the actual aim, but is instead a means to demonstrate that terrors originating within an individual's mind, unassisted by supernaturalism and intoxicants, are as frightening, or more, than those circulated by writers of sleazy tales intended merely to stimulate a tightened gut or cold chills in readers. Poe perceived that he had to write for two audiences. The first, larger group would read his works at face value, relishing what they interpreted as unquestionable supernaturalism. A second, far smaller, more discerning readership would realize that Poe had manipulated conventions of supernatural literature to create subtle psychological fiction (and poetry).

There are, to be sure, other tales that do not fall within the province of Gothic tradition, and it may be useful at this point to examine Poe's non-Gothic works, because the majority of them have a different kind of appeal from that which enlivens those tales that obviously relate to Gothic tradition. When Poe's writings are the topic, however, there must always be some latitude allowed; thus we find several tales that straddle the border between what might be Gothic and what non-Gothic. Among the earliest stories, "A Tale of Jerusalem" (1832) and "Epimanes" ("Four Beasts in One" [1836]) are not Gothic; instead they are more carnivalesque, fashioned by Poe's half-humorous treatment of violence. Violence is principally emotional in "A Tale of Jerusalem." Thinking that their Roman besiegers are sending a lamb or calf for sacrifice, devout Jews are startled to discover a pig instead; shock causes them to drop the basket containing the animal down the walls, unwittingly wreaking havoc below. Whether the Romans had planned a nasty trick or whether they were unaware that eating pork was taboo in Jewish law (as it would not have been for them) is not clarified (*M* 1: 41). The confusion over animals and humans, and the interesting giraffe motif for the procession of the Syrian monarch Antiochus IV in "Epimanes," make fitting counterparts to the actual giraffes given by the Egyptian Pasha, Mohammed Ali, to the kings of France and England, which serve to link ancient and, for Poe, contemporary aspects of mob scenes, which he deplored. "Lionizing" (1835), "The Man That Was Used Up" (1839), "Why the Little Frenchman Wears His Hand in a Sling" (1839) and "The Business Man" (1840) are satiric, but not Gothic, tales.

Another type of tale or sketch, prepared to accompany single-plate illustrations, may be found in "The Island of the Fay" (1841), "Morning on the Wissahiccon" ("The Elk" [1844]) and "Byron and Miss Chaworth" (1844), or in several others that do not include letterpress for plate illustrations but which are prose-poems that portray appealing interior or, more frequently, landscape scenes: "Philosophy of Furniture" (1840), "The Landscape Garden" (1842), "The Domain of Arnheim" (1847) and "Landor's Cottage" (1849). Vision is paramount in these pieces, and the pleasant features in all would have pleased many of Poe's readers. The wealth of description in these writings hardly departs from what we find elsewhere in Poe's prose fiction. If some readers think that description is overdone in Poe's tales, a word from him may make them reconsider. When in "How To Write a Blackwood Article" Mr. Blackwood, the seasoned editor, tells aspirant writer Signora Psyche Zenobia that "Sensations are the great things after all" (*M* 1: 340), his succinct statement might stand as a key to most of Poe's creative works, because it offers a terse but sound theory of symbolism. Poe supplies many "things" as outward forms for spiritual facts, to paraphrase Ralph Waldo Emerson, whose notions of symbolism produced intense reactions, pro or con, among his contemporaries and on through later generations. Visual enticements in all these works serve as keys to inner thoughts. These tales would have appealed to the fad for landscape to which many Americans at the time devoted themselves, so in publishing such sketches Poe appealed to a timely fashion rather than filling pages with what readers would have deemed outré or distasteful.

Still another type of tale, that in which Poe addressed some issue of widespread interest, is represented by "The Unparalleled Adventures of Hans Pfaal" (1835) and companion reading for it, "The Balloon Hoax" (1844). Balloon travel was then much in the public mind, and these tales are Poe's attempts to capitalize on that popular theme while never forswearing his sense of humor. The same may be said of "Some Words with a Mummy" (1845), a tale that satirized the Egyptology fad then sweeping America. Another area in which, of course, Poe had great interest was the contemporary literary marketplace. "Lionizing" (1835), "The Literary Life of Thingum Bob, Esq." (1844) and "X-ing a Paragrab" (1849) are respective hits at certain prominent persons in British literary circles, the Anglo-American magazine world, and editorial practices, or malpractices, that Poe knew only too well.

Some readers have attempted to distinguish Poe's detective or, as he preferred, "ratiocinative" tales from his other fiction, contending that the five, tales of detection, perhaps six if one includes "The Man of the Crowd" (1840), show a strong departure in method from the other fiction he published, particularly since the ratiocinative tales offer a realism that is lacking in most of Poe's other stories. That is a mistaken idea (and a mistaken conception of realism) because the first detective tale, "The Murders in the Rue Morgue" (1841), demonstrates how Poe transformed the Gothic story, with its hints of supernatural causes for the deaths of the L'Espanaye women, into the modern detective story. The apparently supernatural machinations in "Murders," thanks to solutions provided by the canny French sleuth C. A. Dupin, ultimately prove to have very real-life origins. So the techniques in these tales differ little, if at all, from those in his other fiction. To address the other Dupin tales, and "The Gold-Bug" (1843) in which Dupin is not featured, any seeming supernatural touches in "The Mystery of Marie Rogêt" (1842–43) and "The Purloined Letter" (1845) dissipate when reasoning is used to arrive at solutions for the mysteries in all these works.

"The Gold-Bug" embodies more of a supernatural aura than the two Dupin tales just named because it foregrounds Jupe's superstitious nature and Legrand's apparent madness – obvious lures for those readers who would relish potentially spooky Gothicism in a remote setting. Characters within the tale and we readers eventually learn, however, that Legrand knowingly perpetrated mystification about himself and the gold bug because others thought that he was mad. To the narrator, who had been suspicious of his friend's sanity, the solution to finding the treasure seemed to emanate from Legrand's disturbed mental state or else from some supernatural force at work behind the scenes. "The Gold-Bug" was placed first in the prize competition sponsored by the Philadelphia *Dollar Newspaper*, and became one of Poe's most popular tales, frequently reprinted during his lifetime and after, because of its American setting, i.e. Sullivan's Island off the coast of South Carolina. There was even an adaptation, by Silas S. Steele, for the stage, *The Gold-Bug, or, The Pirate's Treasure* (*M* 2: 805).

Legrand's name suggests greatness, a trait which bonds him with M. Dupin, an amateur but peerless sleuth, whose mind far surpasses those in the characters surrounding him. Dupin and Legrand perceive more than their companions, whose notions about the mysteries they encounter go nowhere. Legrand and Dupin are adept at enjoying a good joke at the expense of others who are less perceptive than they. If the French name Dupin were pronounced as a word in English, we would hear something like "duping," which is not far distant from this wily sleuth's frame of mind, especially when he discerns that his ideas are being questioned, which arrives at solutions to mysteries that confound others. The way he takes his less perceptive companion, the unnamed narrator in "Murders," through a series of illuminations about the atrocities committed in the L'Espanaye house prompts the narrator to conclude that a madman or a supernatural creature is the murderer. Folklore attributes more than ordinary human strength to the insane, and if no human perpetrated these horrifying murders, why, then, a supernatural being must be the culprit. For Dupin, however, a reasonable solution emerges, which he must explain to his companion. Other touches of ironic humor in "Murders" reinforce the thought that Poe often enjoyed insinuating ironies into his fiction. That the police chief's major suspect is named "Le Bon" ("The Good") heightens irony in the tale. An even greater irony occurs because, despite all signs to the contrary, Dupin alone realizes that a non-human committed the murders. That the murders occur in the Rue Morgue is another irony: there has never been such a street in Paris, and since Poe changed in manuscript the original "Rue Trianon Bas" to "Rue Morgue," or "Street of the Mortuary," he must have been wholly conscious of the irony.

"The Mystery of Marie Rogêt" (1842–43) displays none of the ironies found in "Murders," though an aura of grimness may be proper in an account of bungled abortion, but the third Dupin tale, "The Purloined Letter" (1845), revolves around a contest of wits between Dupin and the minister D— over the whereabouts of the stolen letter. Knowing that the letter may bring down catastrophe for the noble lady who wrote it, and knowing, too, the minute habits and thinking patterns of his antagonist, Dupin plays a clever game of deception to retrieve the letter from the home of D—, where it had been placed in full sight – under the assumption that nobody would think of discovering the object in such a public location. Dupin and D— are possible twins, thus reminding us of mythologies about one twin's ability to fathom the other's thoughts. Dupin's statement about the superiority of poets over mathematicians imparts to him, the poet, a power over D—, the mathematician, who as such lacks the intuitive mindset of Dupin. Moreover, since D— had once done Dupin an injustice, the sleuth is only too eager to redress that wrong. So he anticipates the surprise that will cause D—'s downfall, when the minister discovers that the letter has been (re)purloined and restored to the lady.

Apparently written at about the same time as "The Purloined Letter," "Thou Art the Man" (1844), Poe's parody of the detective story, has been surprisingly overshadowed by the other ratiocinative tales and their critics. This tale gains zest by wordplay on names (as in "Murders") in combination with joking that brings about grim reprisal to the villain. After the murder of Mr. Barnabas Shuttleworthy, a highly respected and very wealthy citizen of Rattleborough, his presumed best friend, Old Charley Goodfellow, tries to fasten blame on young Mr. Pennifeather, nephew of the murdered man. The name of the community, "Rattleborough," implies that the inhabitants are either scatterbrained or else primed for sensationalism. Comic transparencies also inform the major characters' names. Shuttleworthy does not seem to comprehend Goodfellow's true nature. Pennifeather may hint either that the dissipated young man does not handle money wisely, or that he is primed for flight with his uncle's wealth. Goodfellow's name may suggest genuine goodness, but the "fellow" suffix could as readily indicate, as the term once did, that he is an untrustworthy low-life person. His murder of Shuttleworthy and his machinating to place blame on Pennifeather, whom he had come to hate, attest his evil nature. The nameless narrator has, however, divined Goodfellow's true self, which he despises, finds evidence to prove Goodfellow's guilt, and so contrives to force a public confession from him that exonerates Pennifeather, who subsequently becomes a model citizen. Besides being a take-off on Poe's other detective stories, "Thou Art the Man" is the first crime story in which ballistics are used to identify a murderer. As in many other Poe tales, comedy and seriousness intertwine here, and these characteristics have become part of the world of detective fiction.

Moving away from, but not altogether forgetting, what are usually categorized as Poe's detective stories, we may want to allow that the majority of his tales contain crime-detection themes, though not with a recognized sleuth to unravel the mysteries. Readers themselves often become the implicit detectives in engaging Poe's fiction in which crime is present. To cite again "The Assignation," which many readers today would not firmly place as a crime story, we readers are lured into playing sleuth as the narrator moves through a series of bewilderments, all holding out puzzlement (for him and us) that we want to clarify. In the end we probably surpass the narrator, who is not certain about all that has transpired, as we should be. Another crime tale, "The Man of the Crowd" (1840), hints of criminal thought or activity, yet none ever occurs. Comparable with technique in "The Assignation," Poe makes his narrator seem several times to be moving toward an episode of physical violence, yet no violence occurs. This technique recalls Keats's in his famous poem "The Eve of St. Agnes": the lovers have a feast before them, yet they do not partake; physical violence threatens but it never befalls; and sexual consummation seems imminent, but may not be realized (the situation is ambiguous). Overall, both works promise much, but fail to deliver what most readers would anticipate.

"The Man of the Crowd" is powerful psychological literature in its theme of mystery (which is perhaps evil) harbored internally, giving the tale kinship with Nathaniel Hawthorne's intriguing sketch "The Haunted Mind" (1835), where we read that every human heart contains a dungeon of grim secrets. Although Hawthorne's sketch depicts an internalized mode of thought, the narrator in "The Man of the Crowd" is an onlooker at urban scenes, thus making him an excellent specimen of what many critics call the flaneur. In French that word means "an idler," and Poe's narrator seemingly idles as he looks on and pictorializes urban scenes. In fact, early assessment of the flaneur in Poe's writings concentrated on urban situations.[10] Other Poe protagonists fit the flaneur paradigm. A random sampling might include the narrators in "The Assignation," "The Murders in the Rue Morgue" and "The Purloined

Letter." Compare also other Poe protagonists, for example the narrators in "Lionizing," "The Masque of the Red Death" and "The Sphinx" (1846), and, by extension, the narrators in "Epimanes" (1836), "A Predicament" (1838), "William Wilson" (1839), "The Business Man" and "Why the Little Frenchman Wears His Hand in a Sling"(both 1840), as well as those who create a word-picture for readers' focus in such tales as "The Conversation of Eiros and Charmion" (1839), "Raising the Wind" ("Diddling" [1843]),"Morning on the Wissahiccon," "Some Words with a Mummy" and "The Spectacles" (all 1844), "The Sphinx" (1846) and "Mellonta Tauta" (1849). As I have remarked, many of Poe's tales reveal that they are not self-contained, but that instead they overlap in techniques with others (and with the poems). Therefore we might discover flaneur qualities in works that I do not cite. One might well contend that just about all of Poe's tales (and, perhaps, many of the poems, for example "To Helen," "The Valley of Unrest," "The City in the Sea" or "The Coliseum") may be touched with the flaneur motif, and the same may be said about *The Narrative of Arthur Gordon Pym* and *The Journal of Julius Rodman*.

The flaneur character allows writers like Poe to make deft transitions from panoramic to individual scenes, which in turn reflect the psychological makeup of the narrator (and perhaps other characters as well), thus preventing boredom, and the curiosity in such an onlooker enhances the visual element in a tale as he (or she, in "A Predicament") mulls possibilities for meaning in what is beheld, be his/her thoughts the musings of an idler or shock reactions to startling or appalling visual scenes. Ramifications of the flaneur enrich many of Poe's creative writings.

An easy transition takes us to a cluster of tales in which an onlooker-narrator plays a significant role. These tales begin with an air of scientific accuracy that moves on into an increasingly weird conclusion, which seems to link with supernaturalism. In "A Tale of the Ragged Mountains" and "Mesmeric Revelation" (1844) and "The Facts in the Case of M. Valdemar" (1845), it is mesmerism, one of the pseudo-sciences that became a fad in the nineteenth century, which we now call hypnotism. The first of the three tales combines ideas of metempsychosis (transmigration of souls) with mesmeric lore in a manner that had been to some degree adumbrated in "Metzengerstein," and a more recent contention is that vampirism rather than mesmerism brings about the horrible death of Augustus Bedloe, contributing to the multiple appeal in this tale. The other two tales feature a nameless narrator, friend of a tuberculosis victim who is mesmerized to forestall death. Especially in "Valdemar," the theme of the will's capacity to delay the onset of death reminds us of Poe's strong-willed women characters, most notably Ligeia, whose returns wreak havoc in their lovers' psyches (the tales with women's names for titles will be discussed below). "Valdemar" struck many of Poe's contemporaries as utterly repulsive, though he responded that he intended it as a hoax, and hoax aspects should not be discounted in reading the other mesmeric tales. Poe was no enthusiast for many of the scientific, philosophic or political causes that excited many of his contemporaries, but he was assiduous in addressing them, usually with satiric response, in several of his writings.

The widespread interest in millennium predictions underlies several other tales that portray existence in the afterlife. "The Conversation of Eiros and Charmion" (1839), "The Colloquy of Monos and Una" (1841), "The Power of Words" (1845) and "Mellonta Tauta" (1849) are all constructed as dialogues between two characters who have passed through death to immortality. These tales include none of the gruesome medical details that created sensationalism in the mesmeric pieces, though all may be labeled "science fiction" (along with several others). The characters often articulate critiques of nineteenth-century society and its beliefs. The pair in the first derive names from characters in Shakespeare's *Antony and Cleopatra*, a drama about love, but not domestic love. The coming of the comet, which wreaks destruction, promotes interest in reason, but, as Dupin would make evident, reason alone does not lead to ultimate truth. The "colloquy" in the second tale argues for greater latitude in understanding art and the function of artists. Oinos and Agathos, in "The Power of Words," engage what amounts to a Romantic viewpoint regarding symbolism, in which the symbol functions as metaphor far more emphatically than as simile. But, then, the characters' names respectively mean *one* or *wine*, and *good*, so Poe may insinuate that the power of some of the words, at least, in this tale was not without mirth. After all, in "Tales of the Folio Club" the criticism tendered involved satire upon then current critical outlooks. Humor, though it is biting, underlies an attack on nineteenth-century life, most particularly on the urban scene. Structuring these tales as dialogues would, of course, initially give them an air of dignity, but Poe's love of fooling knew no bounds, even amidst such gravity.

"Silence – A Fable" and "Shadow – A Parable" might also qualify as apocalyptic-science fiction, but underlying comic features, perhaps (but only perhaps) of greater import in the second of these tales, should caution us against seeing nothing more than solemn contexts in both tales. "Silence – A Fable" has already been discussed as being, in one version at least, a tale read by one drunken Folio Club member to equally drunken listeners, thereby accounting for the extravagant sound effects. Transplanted from "Tales of the Folio Club," "Silence – A Fable" may parallel an extrasensory or paranormal experience that permits transitions between one world and another. Here and in "Shadow – A Parable" the intersection of comedy with sobriety is so cleverly wrought that distinguishing one from the other proves difficult. Of course, why shouldn't readers sustain puzzlement – since characters within each tale continue to be baffled by what they witness?

The apocalyptic features in "Shadow – A Parable," another tale redolent of biblical language structures, are appropriate for the funereal occasion at hand. Nonetheless, we may divine comedy lying just below the biblical cadences. As a narrative related by Oinos (whose name may mean "wine," as well as "one"), this tale of a group's ostensibly assembling to pay final respects to their dead comrade, the "young Zoilus," may recapitulate the Folio Club's concluding debacle just a little too closely to ignore. The historical Zoilus was a carping critic in ancient Greece, whose criticism of Homer was notably fault-finding. Zoilus in "Shadow – A Parable" has fallen victim to the plague raging locally, his mourners betray hysterical laughter alternating with fear – natural reactions from those who have seen the plague depopulate their community, and who may also at any moment be stricken. They drink repeatedly to soothe themselves, though the eventual arrival of Shadow (of death, as he seems to be to this group) frightens them. With its situations paralleling those in the Folio Club – laughter mingled with grimness, a critic (whose name is that of a historical person and a nickname for Poe, the quondam unduly harsh critic in the *Messenger*) dead from the plague, which in this tale may hint of the deadly personalities and circumstances within the Folio Club – "Shadow – A Parable" is an original tale mingling fears with mirth, detailing overmuch consumption of wine (likewise prominent in the Folio Club), and a conclusion rife with bewilderment (which could also, little retouched, function as the rout in the Folio Club) so maneuvered as to approximate figurative death for the pretenses of that organization when public exposure occurs.

Poe's sea fiction, "MS. Found in a Bottle," *The Narrative of Arthur Gordon Pym*, "A Descent into the Maelström" (1841) and "The Oblong Box" (1844), represents another bid for popularity, whatever other intentions may inform these works, and although *Pym* did not gain kudos during Poe's lifetime it has since been acclaimed as one of his greatest imaginative works. Sea fiction featuring sensational episodes had won admiration throughout the Anglo-American literary world; therefore once again Poe's turning to a type of writing that might financially reward him materialized in works far exceeding run-of-the-mill quality. "MS. Found" has been reprinted in many collections of sea, adventure and mystery stories. That popularity bears witness to Poe's accomplishments in the suspense story; the narrator's gradual succumbing to ever more fantastic and overpowering forces at sea culminates in the climax of his descent in a whirlpool to the bottom of the sea or into the interior of the earth, either possibility bringing literal or metaphoric death to him. This story may also be read as a symbolic journey into the depths of the self, which has terrifying aspects. Transgressing the bounds of rationality may be exciting, as the narrator in "MS. Found" discovers, but there may be astonishing, and unpleasant, revelations in store for the person who travels into unfamiliar worlds of the emotions. Similar negations of rational thought gain greater dimension in many of Poe's other tales (and in poems like "The Raven," "Ulalume" and "Annabel Lee"). The same might be said of "A Descent into the Maelström" or *The Narrative of Arthur Gordon Pym* (the latter will be addressed later in this chapter).

"A Descent into the Maelström" (1841) obviously appealed to nineteenth-century readers, if reprints and several translations into French are barometers of its popularity (*M* 1: 577). Although Poe's spiral-whirlpool motif might lead readers to anticipate that they would find in "A Descent" repetition of the conclusions in "MS. Found" and *Pym*, Poe devised an inversion technique. The narrator does descend into the great whirlpool, as if he will go to his death in the bottom of the ocean. He is, however, miraculously spiraled upward to the surface by a counter-movement in the great whirlpool, though his frame of mind has been unalterably disturbed. Whatever his outlook, he minutely details the action and effects of the great whirlpool, and he has been so strongly impressed by his near death that he feels compulsion to retell his story. Poe's character is thus a literary relative of Coleridge's ancient mariner, who was also caught up by mysterious forces at sea, never to be the same man again. The plunge and resurfacing of Poe's mariner do not occur with seeming rapidity; rather, "A Descent" stands as a perfect tale in which sensations are paramount, and the chronicling of his sensations seems to be essential to the narrator. He numbers among the extremely few Poe protagonists who are not dead or dying as their adventures conclude.

"The Oblong Box" (1844) recounts a wonderful build-up of suspense aboard ship as the narrator's misapprehensions of a relationship between two other characters intensify until a startling truth is revealed: the presumed "wife" of Mr. Wyatt turns out to be her maid because his wife has died and he has been attempting to transport her body, in the oblong box, so her mother can participate in her funeral. Perhaps "The Oblong Box" is one among several recyclings by Poe of materials that he had previously used. In part we may consider this tale as detective fiction, but if we do so we must rank it with others in which the sleuth fails, for example Inspector Bucket in Charles Dickens's *Bleak House* (1852) or Sergeant Cuff in Wilkie Collins's *The Moonstone* (1868). For that matter, Poe's own Dupin might have failed in clearing up the precise causes of Marie Rogêt's death, had Poe not broken the monthly sequence of that tale in *Snowden's Ladies' Companion*, where installments appeared in November and December 1842, followed by a break in January, the final installment appearing only in February 1843. As background for this tale, Poe had depended closely on newspaper accounts of Mary Rogers's disappearance and death (the real-life model for Marie). When what were (to Poe) unexpected reasons for the actual death were pointed out, he had to alter his story. His predilections for ciphers may lurk in the background of this tale, although, as was true in his commentary on Dickens's *Barnaby Rudge*, Poe had not arrived at an actual solution for Marie's mysterious death when he began or even when he had drafted much of the tale. Poe's relish of cryptography may also reside in backgrounds for the other ratiocinative pieces, since those tales and the cryptographic articles appeared during the early 1840s.

Several other tales are best viewed as a cluster in which two significant principles are paramount: (a) the concept of doubles/twins or (b) that of a strong feminine presence. There are, of course, certain overlappings between these themes, just as other overlappings occur elsewhere within the canon. An interest in twins was by no means unique to Poe, who, we might say, inherited that interest as part of Romantic tradition. The idea that two persons could be so closely related that, in certain instances, they think and act identically, or nearly so, held out great fascination for the Romantic temperament. Even when two persons were not literally twins from a single womb, the concept of two natures linked by some common thread intrigued many during this era of embryonic psychological study.

In treating doublings, we must return to "Metzengerstein," where the young Baron's humanity yields ultimately to the ungovernable power exemplified in the great fiery horse. One might say that the rider becomes symbolically married to his horse, who is also his nemesis, or that Frederick and the horse are twin halves, one human (if not humane), the other animal(-istic), of a single self. In this context the horse may plausibly be the young man's evil twin or other. Their union occurs, of course, not just to fulfill a prophecy that forecasts evil for the Metzengerstein family, which in Poe's day would have been all too "German" – only that and nothing more. Symbolically, and more significantly, the bonding suggests that Frederick's nature partakes of beastly, i.e. uncontrollable or irrational, depths, fittingly represented by the horse and the fire associated with the animal. Long tradition has characterized horses as intensely sexual (compare the centaur that occurs in Classical mythology). Connecting the horse with fire enhances that association in terms of sexual and other "heat," which may be exciting but also destructive. As the tale closes, Frederick cannot choose but remain in the saddle, the horse having overpowered the young man's volition. We might say that the horse was the victor in a contest of wills. Horse and rider's disappearance amidst sensational tempest and fire fittingly concludes this tale, which ending may also adumbrate the apocalyptic dialogues mentioned above.

At what we might call the mere Gothic surface of the tale, Frederick's disappearance amidst the conflagration, spirited away by a horse, would appeal to that segment of Poe's readers who were all too ready to suppose that hellfire and damnation would be the portion of such profligates as young Metzengerstein. Moreover, if Frederick destroyed the tangible part of the Berlifitzing family and estate by fire, then his own demise ironically parallels that destruction. Poe may also have modified a bit of folklore in this episode. Whereas Satan was often supposed to arrive on a great black horse to claim his victims, the human pigmentation of the giant steed is a deft alteration by Poe's own imaginative vision. And although "Metzengerstein" may not have been written first among Poe's tales, its content undeniably looks forward to much else in the fiction and later poems. Frederick's circumstances remind us to glance again at Poe's Tamerlane, though the Asian military scourge's ambitions had no supernatural assistance. Frederick's plight also anticipates what occurs in "The Black Cat" and "The Raven," plus variations on the theme elsewhere in the canon.

The much more obvious twin relationship in "William Wilson" shows Poe's advance in handling doubles. Not only do the two William Wilsons look alike; even more striking, their names are identical. Just as important, the narrator names himself, just as Ishmael does in Herman Melville's *Moby-Dick* (1851). The Wilsons' names also ensure our remembering that the theme of will is foremost in this tale (Will, I am, will's son), and that will as a subject recurs often in Poe's creative writings. To minimize confusion here, I refer to the narrator as Wilson 1 and the second William Wilson as Wilson 2. Drawing upon memories of his years in the Reverend John Bransby's school at Stoke Newington, near London, Poe rightly created a tale of learning/becoming educated about human will. Wilson 1 does not profit in any intended way during his school years or those which follow, though he does learn, bit by bit, about his own will, of which, however, Wilson 2 represents an integral force. The windings and darkened interiors in this tale are excellent signposts for the similar journeying within his own mind that Wilson 1 engages throughout. In like manner Wilson 2 appears only in shadowy scenes, and speaks in a correspondingly indistinct tone, because Wilson 1 wishes to ignore his double's, i.e. conscience's, counsel. This unwillingness to heed sound advice resembles the similar response of the narrator to Psyche in "Ulalume." The profligacy of Wilson 1 heightens till he reaches desperation, losing control of all rationality. His confrontation with Wilson 2, whom he stabs while they both stand before a mirror, is an excellent technique of Poe's because all the while Wilson 1, in looking at Wilson 2, is analogous to one's gazing into a mirror, which shows an inexact reflection. Reflection, i.e. looking back or, in context, condescending, characterizes the stance of Wilson 1 in his relationship with Wilson 2. When they finally confront directly, as it were, Wilson 1, driven to rage and despair, cannot refrain from stabbing himself (or his self, no matter the customarily ungrammatical usage). Wilson 1 cannot live without conscience, a major component in his will, even if he has long tried to shut his ears to its voice. Wilson 1's recounting of these gloomy circumstances may be his attempt to bring coherence to what have been essentially chaotic events in his life – his physically active life and, more important, his mental life. "William Wilson" resembles many other *Bildungsroman* fictions, though Wilson 1's maturing/learning is an inversion of the more usual portrait, i.e. here the protagonist ends in a degenerate instead of a regenerate state. Poe reworked this plot line in "The Raven," where he substituted for the sensational murder at the close of "William Wilson" an emphatic stillness of voice and volition in the speaker and the raven. One might think, reasonably, that William Wilson 1 has likewise been reduced to silence. Ironically, his own speaking voice, like that of his double, has been destroyed, so he resumes "speaking," as it were, with aid of paper and pen.

A tale that in several features might be a recycling of "William Wilson," "The Cask of Amontillado," has spawned readings that extend from its possible biographical origins (Poe's "revenge" upon T. D. English for the latter's libel and the lawsuit, where Poe came out the winner) to its being a tale of the perfect crime, or a fictionalizing of Roman Catholic–Masonic enmity. Understandably, names are significant in "Cask." To Poe's contemporaries, Montresor might have been reminiscent of John Montrésor, a British engineer, presumably the original of Montraville, Charlotte's seducer in Susannah H. Rowson's famous novel *Charlotte Temple* (1794). Fortunato's name means "the fortunate one" or "the fated one" (*M* 2: 1255–56), and trying to decide just which implication obtains is frustrating (providing another example of multiple, equally valid possibilities in one of Poe's writings). In light of this and other elements of multiple intent in the tale, Poe's revising the name of a third character, who never appears, should make us all the more attentive to implications in Poe's namings/characterizations. In the first version of "The Cask of Amontillado," in *Godey's* for November 1846, this third character, Luchresi, is mentioned knowingly by Montresor in an implicit appeal to Fortunato's knowledge of wines. If Luchresi, like Dupin's ironic name, is one that in English sounds like "look crazy," that phrase might be wordplay on the ambiguities and deceptions that course through this tale. The revision to "Luchesi" might be construed as Poe's attempt to tone down extravagance; on the other hand, that name also sounds like two English words, "look hazy," and "Cask" is hazy indeed in its never quite yielding up any single meaning, particularly in terms of characterization.

Montresor's motive for murdering Fortunato has been much debated, but the most likely reading is one that sees Montresor as an evil principle, Fortunato the good, in a self. So their journey into the cellars of Montresor's palace represents a descent into the depths of the self, where the murder functions as a suppression of the good component within the self. The overarching irony is, however, Montresor's failure to evade a significant part of himself (his self). His suppressive desires rebound on him, and even though he returns to semblances of a normal life, he cannot escape a fate that binds him to Fortunato. If Montresor has buried, i.e. repressed, the "fortunate" part of his being, he becomes fated never to forget that event. Therefore he relates a narrative – one of the most wonderfully detailed among Poe's tales – in which he relives the crime, so bound by his memories that he clearly reproduces the dialogue from that long-past event. Fortunato may not return in ghostly form to torment Montresor, but his impact is nonetheless inescapable.

One might also look at this chronicle of twin halves of what should be an integrated self as a work of historical fiction. Just as "The Murders in the Rue Morgue" capitalized on the then timely establishment of police detection (against which, however, Poe plays off a more clever amateur sleuth), so certain historical factors enrich "Cask." For example, Montresor's cloak, a roquelaire, sets this story during the later eighteenth century, when that garb was introduced into western Europe and became fashionable men's wear. That time frame should also lead us to consider attentively the dialogue involving "the love of God," voiced by Montresor and Fortunato near the conclusion. Previously, the two had commented on Masonic tokens. Their exchanges induced Montresor, responding to Fortunato's hand motion (apparently a Masonic gesture), to produce a stonemason's trowel, in what may be a telling allusion to the nature of Montresor's enmity toward his comrade. If Fortunato belonged to the Masonic fraternity, he would have been an enemy to devout Roman Catholics. In the late eighteenth century, the Masonic brotherhood struck from their rituals all specific references to Christ, which action brought down upon the Masons great hostility from Roman Catholicism. Since "Cask" is set in southwestern Europe, where the Roman Catholic church exercised vast power at the time, Montresor's move against Fortunato would be understandable, if exaggerated by Poe. The walling up of Fortunato would be a supremely ironic means for ridding the world of a Mason, i.e. a heretic. Consequently Montresor deems his murder justified for "the love of God," though Montresor's love negates compassion and charity.

More may be involved with the phrase used by the two men. To Fortunato, Montresor's chaining him fast seems at first to be a joke, and so he naturally responds, "Let us be gone." Montresor repeats that sentence, but his articulation of those words is mockery of his victim. What Montresor does not realize, but what the tale bears out, is that he also becomes "gone" (or dead, literally and figuratively), gone specifically for the love of God. Montresor may commit murder, as he thinks, to satisfy God, but in killing Fortunato he also murders part of himself, which killing amounts to suicide, a sin against God according to Christian doctrine.

No wonder, then, that this murderer remains so clear as to details of his crime. That event has affected the rest of his life, and if, as some readings submit, he is now making a deathbed confession to a priest ("You, who so well know the nature of my soul" – *M* 2: 1256), during which he reveals his transgression, he would naturally be doubtful about salvation. Montresor is damned because a fatal slip reveals that he was not so cold-blooded as most of his account might suggest. Realizing that Fortunato may have fainted when he comprehended the enormity of his situation, Montresor recollects: "My heart grew sick – on account of the dampness of the catacombs" (*M* 2: 1263). This hesitancy stands as a classic Freudian slip; half a century later he cannot refrain from blurting out the truth – in an old man's fragile moment, perhaps? – though he quickly tries to cover up that blunder. Having once blundered, however, Montresor commits another, similar slip in his final words. Does he invoke the Latin from the Roman Catholic burial service for the sake of Fortunato, thus speaking ironically, or, in a voice of truth, does he invoke it for his own future? We will never know.

"The Cask of Amontillado" is another of Poe's crime tales in which crime against one's self is the actual concern, making this tale a stellar achievement in psychological fiction. The dialogue ranks as one of Poe's outstanding technical successes, both in the ironies that permeate the verbal exchanges (and several of Montresor's asides) and in its dramatic strength. Indeed the tale exemplifies Poe's excellences in creating dramatic effects in his fiction (and poems), no matter that he fell short when he assayed drama itself. A first-rate film could be designed without any departures from Poe's text. Understandably, "Cask" serves as a perennial anthology selection; its appeal is undoubted, probably because of the numerous possibilities it offers for interpretation (if one reads out of rather than into the text).

Of equal interest is a group of tales in which the double for the male protagonist-narrator is a female, as if Poe was harking back to the ancient belief that a single being possessed female and male characteristics. In Poe's fiction, couples sometimes seem to be twinned, literally with Roderick and

Madeline Usher, though there the pair are not spouses but siblings. The first of these tales, "Berenice" (1835), was deplored as being too horrible, and White remonstrated with Poe over the content. Poe justified his motives for writing "Berenice" and for sending it to White. Admitting that the tale was "far too horrible" (*O* 57), he emphasized that it was nonetheless fiction that would sell and attract attention to the *Messenger* because magazines "which have attained celebrity were indebted for it to articles similar in nature – to Berenice – although, I grant you far superior in style and execution." Poe goes on to explain that the nature of such fiction is to display "the ludicrous heightened into the grotesque: the fearful into the horrible: the witty exaggerated into the burlesque: the singular wrought out into the strange and mystical . . . To be appreciated you must be read, and these things are invariably sought after with avidity." He concludes this justification by stating that tales of this variety attract readers and so "augment the reputation of the source where they originated." Here Poe demonstrates his own keen awareness of his literary milieu, pointing chiefly to what typified many literary periodicals and the nature of marketable fiction.

Berenice and the narrator, her cousin, are betrothed, but she falls ill from a mysterious disease, presumably dies, and is buried. The narrator is fixated on her teeth, and the more her physical beauty deteriorates, the more prominent they become. He opens her grave, and pulls her teeth – only to learn, after succumbing to a trance state, that Berenice was actually alive when he pulled the teeth, but that she died from the trauma of that violence. Not accidentally is this narrator named Egaeus, the same name as Hermia's father in Shakespeare's *A Midsummer Night's Dream*, a man who does not comprehend the nature of love, and whose spiritual handicap almost causes tragedy. Poe's Egaeus tells us that he was born in a library, which still serves as the vital center of his life. His mother had died there – implicitly, Egaeus' living quarters were death-dealing to women. He rapidly loses his love for Berenice because her physical appearance seems increasingly to repel him. Whether her physical features actually turn repulsive, or whether Egaeus falsifies (to rationalize his avoidance of marrying and, presumably, engaging with what should be the emotional and physical intimacy in marriage) is never made clear.

Bereft of Berenice, Egaeus himself deteriorates spiritually, thus prompting his violation of her grave. Unlike several other women in Poe's writings who sicken and die, Berenice does not return to persecute this lover, whose own ego had apparently killed any emotional bonding between them, though rec-ollections of her haunt Egaeus, as is evident throughout the tale. Emotionally disoriented, he disjointedly describes the burial of Berenice, which torments him with a memory "replete with horror – horror more horrible from being vague, and terror more terrible from ambiguity. It was a fearful page in the record of my existence, written all over with dim, and hideous, and unintelligible recollections" (*M* 2: 217–18). Aware that these hazy memories are connected with a "shrill and piercing shriek of a female voice" (*M* 2: 218), Egaeus continues to grope for meaning in what he remembers, until a servant enters to announce that Berenice's grave has been desecrated. Egaeus then discovers his own dishevelment, and knocks down a small box he has been regarding uneasily. The suspense, which has been carefully built up, culminates when the box smashes and Berenice's teeth scatter over the floor.

Although many readers find "Berenice" too gruesome, Poe's success lay in the deft mingling of surface repulsiveness with Egaeus' inward-turning emotions. Consequently the tale moves beyond mere cardboard characterization coupled with facile sensationalism, which, as Poe modifies these features, may not be extravagances after all, because they filter to us through Egaeus' disintegrating consciousness. Thus Poe creates a psychologically realistic tale. Egaeus' "I found myself" (*M* 2: 217), when he returns to the library after finishing his atrocious assault on Berenice's teeth, subtly but convincingly implies that he functions better in this room than he does elsewhere because his mind is at its greatest ease (which is, however, no placid ease) within that interior space, than it is when he ventures beyond such confines. Egaeus is a notable case of one so restricted by an interiorized world that he develops an antipathy to the world beyond those confines, and to the physical manifestations that are part of that world. So he cannot help but create disaster, for Berenice and – since she is part of his being, whether he is at ease with that union or not – for himself.

One might see a direct line extending, for example, from Egaeus to Adam Stanton, in Robert Penn Warren's novel *All the King's Men* (1946). Adam is a physician whose code of life is supremely idealistic (his name is a transparency) until he learns of his sister Anne's affair with Governor Willie Stark, who has seemed to be a great friend to the siblings. Shock reaction motivates Adam's gunning down of Stark and being shot to death himself by Stark's bodyguards. An interesting reversal, in which the man of action attempts to play an ideal role but finally reverts to animal viciousness and murder, exists in Frank Norris's brutish dentist in the novel *McTeague* (1899). Western world literature after Poe produced a long line of characters, usually though not exclusively the protagonists in the work where they appear, whose attempts to be what they are not brings about disaster for themselves and others. One notable character who seems outwardly to be a man of ideals, but who capitalizes on his pretense, is John Jasper, in Dickens's *The Mystery of Edwin Drood* (1870), whose dual personality is destructive to his own emotional life and probably sexually violent and even murderous to several others. Many characters in Eugene O'Neill's plays also come to mind in such contexts, because they move on a descending trajectory from noble ideals to horrifying ill will toward others, thence to murderous urges. Orin Mannon, in *Mourning Becomes Electra* (1934), is just such a type. His youthful, wholesome outlook on life comes to be tainted by his incestuous feelings toward his mother and sister, turning him into the murderer of the women's shared lover and later to his own suicide.

Another look at "Berenice" may intimate Poe's possible comic intent while composing this tale. Egaeus' origins, which, he tells us, are literary – born in a library, named for a Shakespeare character – may place him as a stereo-typical Gothic protagonist, or as one prone to observe life through a Gothic lens, implied by his predilections for gloom, whether he is describing persons, places or thoughts. Therefore his love relationship may be doomed from the start; doomed love affairs are frequent in Gothic tradition, albeit many Goth-ics conclude with some lovers finding happiness. That doomedness would make plausible Egaeus' unstable feelings toward Berenice and the consequent horrible occurrences. Add a live burial, a gruesome grave robbing and the con-comitant torture inflicted on a still-living being, and we have all the features of much that is considered to be Gothic (in Poe's day, "German"). Moreover, just as Poe elsewhere fashions surface sensations that hint at more interior impor-tance, Berenice may represent the more sane, potentially creative, even earthy elements in the self she could share with Egaeus, did not his own destructive impulses negate that potential.

As is typical of his practices, Poe's revisions to "Berenice" demonstrate great care in rechanneling even the most lurid circumstances toward greater plausibility. So we are left once again to ponder the nature of fixed mean-ing. Even in this early tale, Poe may be seen as a forerunner of later exis-tentialist thought in his delineation of fragmented sensibilities and (in some respects, at least) inconclusive endings for his imaginative works. Such indeci-siveness as grips Poe's protagonists may indeed result from the terror of the soul which, Poe stated, he had aimed to portray, rather than the mere "German" gloom which his critics, accurately or not, deplored as typifying several of his tales.

Less horrid in outreach, "Morella," in the *Messenger* for May 1835, which followed close upon the publication of "Berenice" the previous month, might suggest that Poe's literary imagination was intent upon producing tales in which female characters possessed a dynamism lacking in their male survivors/storytellers. In this second tale we find a far greater emphasis upon will than in "Berenice." Now Poe reworked the theme of metempsy-chosis, or transmigration of souls, that he had advantageously employed in "Metzengerstein," and that he would continue to use elsewhere, for example in "A Tale of the Ragged Mountains." Poe adroitly introduces possibilities of magic or witchcraft into "Morella"; the wife's will has such binding force upon her husband's will that, as he senses the circumstances, a magic spell seems to be at work. We might find that their marriage is analogous to that of the young couple in Hawthorne's "Young Goodman Brown," where the husband cannot, even temporarily, without uneasiness depart from Faith, whose transparent name encompasses his religious beliefs, which have been his philosophy of life, without sustaining a severe shock. Furthermore, what he had anticipated as somewhat plausible eventuates in a severely negative jolt to his sensibilities, from which he never recovers.

Morella dies in childbirth, though her will lives on in her daughter, whose identity replicates that of the mother. After ten years have passed, the father's decision to have his child baptized with the mother's name brings about catastrophe. When he names the child to the priest, the girl collapses with the words, "I am here!" – then dies, as if she is responding to the summons from a voice beyond the grave. When the father takes her corpse to the tomb he finds no trace of the mother's body, which, of course, could have disintegrated with time's passage. In keeping with the predominance of the first Morella's will, though, what haunts the survivor originates far more in an emotional than a physical presence, reinforcing the theme of will. The indistinct figures and the shadows that contribute to the narrator's fixity on Morella are first-rate phenomena for emphasizing mind rather than tangibles. In Jungian psychology a shadow represents the "other," the unpredictable element in self.

Overall, repetitions of Morella's name act hypnotically on the narrator, while they make lyrical prose that enchants readers (i.e. sings them, as it were, into the world and events within the weird tale). "Morella" is a fine example of Poe's carrying over into his prose fiction the lyrical effects more often associated with poetry. The poet's chief aim is to use verbal powers to persuade audiences into accepting, temporarily of course, the world and the inhabitants of that world within a poem. Poe's often lyrical tales exemplify another trend fostered by many other Romantic writers, that of composing poetic prose. It might be more to the point here to say, as regards "Morella," that Poe's technique in enchanting (chanting–repeating–hypnotizing us into the world of this or any other individual tale or poem) is his means of willing us to be attentive to the situation in this tale, just as he has done elsewhere, for example in "King Pest" or "Lionizing" or (perhaps somewhat more stridently) in "Silence – A Fable."

"Ligeia," which Poe ranked as his best tale, has invited many readings, including interpreting it as a fiction in which genuine supernaturalism makes it a weird tale by an insane narrator, albeit other opinions have been volunteered.

The mad-narrator theory may spring from knowledge that the main inspiration for "Ligeia" was Dickens's "A Madman's Manuscript," from *The Pickwick Papers* (1836–37), which tale Poe reprinted entire as part of a review in the *Messenger* for November 1836. Ligeia herself is another of Poe's female characters whose will is so powerful and dominant that they seem almost superhuman, as well as supernatural. Perhaps the impact of that strong will so envelops the narrator, her survivor, that he can no longer recall just where they met (except that they met in some German city on the Rhine) or Ligeia's family name – nor much else other than her classic features, which may be a rewrite of his earlier Helen's, saving that Ligeia's hair is "raven black" while painters have usually depicted Helen of Troy as fair and light-haired.

Early in the tale, Ligeia's face conveys a radiance similar to the more general, abstract radiance associated with Helen in Poe's poem; all of his characters with names derivative from the same stem as Helen – Lenore, Eleonora – and even some without such names, (for example the Marchesa Aphrodite in "The Assignation," and, in part, Ligeia herself) are surrounded by or associated with radiant light. Thus Lenore in "The Raven" is a "rare and radiant maiden," named by the angels no less, and in "The Assignation" we are twice led to scenes where the Marchesa appears surrounded by dazzling light. Her name, taken from the Goddess Aphrodite, even more closely connects her with light because painters picture that goddess with shining light as background. Likening Ligeia's beauty to that of the Daughters of Delos alludes to the Classical legend of the island sacred to Apollo (to whom allusion is made in Poe's tale) and Artemis, both deities connected with light, respectively that of the sun and the moon. Poe's familiarity with astrological lore was often used to advantage in his creative writings, as it is in "The Sleeper" or "Ulalume."

Ligeia's beauty is not without strangeness, and that strangeness may link up with her preeminent will and her movements being likened to those of a shadow. Again the shadow seems to be that of the narrator's double or inner "other," a double who functions as the less rational part of the human mind or self. Therefore the narrator's mentioning his soul in the opening sentence may signify strong, if not conscious, motivation, from more imaginative than rational impulses. Consequently we should not find surprising his later confusion over the identities of Rowena and Ligeia. If in fact each of these females represents some aspect of his own personality, the conclusion to the tale strongly hints that inner forces, not externals (Rowena seems to exist wholly in external planes), are primary in life. In other words, the narrator marries Ligeia because he is impressed by her mind, as indicated by his dwelling on her face (which houses her mind/will) and her eyes (which in legend are windows into the mind/soul) when he describes her.

His eventual disenchantment with so much mind leads to Ligeia's corporeal death, though she apprises him that death of the body does not necessarily mean a corresponding death of the will. After her death, in what could be a perfectly understandable reaction, the narrator, in a fit of perversity, marries Rowena, who for him may be the epitome of physical allure. His perversity is an inherent trait, but one that provides a key to much in this tale. He purchases in a remote area in rural England a most uninviting abbey with a bridal chamber designed as a pentagon (in folklore a shape linked with magic). To this house the narrator, now a confirmed opium addict, brings Rowena, whom he actually despises (he seems to have an aversion to the physical and, perhaps, to sex), and there he subjects her to psychological tortures. She rapidly grows ill, wastes away to a deathlike state, but ultimately terrifies the narrator because the figure who became sick as Rowena turns out to be Ligeia, proving that will survives physical death, and that any attempt to repress strong emotional forces may lead to terrifying fantasies. The narrator in "Ligeia" is nothing if we bypass his fantasies.

"Ligeia" is another of Poe's renderings of suppression of strong emotional forces, which will in the end well up to create mental turmoil. The male and female characters make clearer for readers the suggestions within this tale, or, to resort to colloquialism, they give us handles to inward states of mind. The confining architecture that is detailed and the deathliness fostered by such restriction are excellent symbols for a human mind that excludes what is emotionally healthy; in fact the narrator earlier refers to his "closed study" (*M* 2: 311), as if to confirm from the start his own closed-mindedness. No wonder that so much illness, dream vision and death occupy "Ligeia." The narrator's turning from one wife to another may symbolize a shift from desire for mind to desire for physical attractiveness/sex, but Rowena's attractions soon prove dissatisfying, as indicated by the brief period till she sickens. The husband had, of course, already created the honeymoon chamber to impress a ghastliness upon anyone entering, but he and Rowena seem to be the only inhabitants of that dreadful room, as if in making that the main site of their marriage he has deliberately set the stage for a ghoulish future – which indeed proves to be his lot.

His establishment of this weird bridal chamber is a pictorial revelation of his own warped mind, as much as it may be the trappings in an impressive supernatural story. This is an inversion of what many would call a dream home. Thus Poe's manipulation of conventional supernatural fiction to serve his own greater art is well carried out. The old Gothic castle or abbey is made to work in new ways, creating a symbolic structure that is pathetically lacking in many other Gothic works composed solely to convey quick thrills. The traditional pair of harassed lovers also reappears in new guise; they are fashioned not as mere cardboard figures but as cornerstone emblems of psychological literature. The conclusion operates on the narrator and on readers alike as the climax of a hideous nightmare. The tale opens with apparent credibility, which is thoroughly undermined, bit by bit, as the narrator's chronicle of his marriages veers from plausibility (e.g. the Rhine area of Germany, an abbey in rural England) into an overwhelming fantasy. That "Ligeia" concludes in a manner that resembles the ending of a nightmare is wholly appropriate – the dream has ended, and there is no more to follow. In certain respects, i.e. the narrator's two wives, "Ligeia" might well be a contemporary story for our era of successive, temporary marriages and the fragile emotions that are parts of those brief unions. The narrator-husband may also operate as a serial killer (in eliminating his wives), a feature in this tale that certainly can speak strongly to twenty-first-century readers.

Even more successful, perhaps, as the portrayal of a disintegrating mind, "The Fall of the House of Usher" (1839) returns us to the motif of twins, in this case a brother and sister whose existence is bound up in each other and with their "house" – the stone mansion and the concept of house as a people/family or mind. Mabbott rightly designates "Usher" as one of "Poe's earlier tales of wonder" (*M* 2: 392), because wonders do seem to infiltrate what the narrator relates. He also seems to wonder about what he beholds, though he never arrives at any satisfactory conclusions. Recalling "Ligeia" and "Morella," three major characters appear in this tale, though many readers forget that the narrator's role has any importance, just as many readers of Herman Melville's *Moby-Dick* seem to overlook the centrality of narrator-Ishmael in that book. I contend at the outset that what Poe achieves in "Usher" is a dramatization of the narrator's collapsing mind, and that his entry into the Usher mansion is analogous to entering his own interior self, that Roderick and Madeline are figures who frighten him because they mirror his own emotional and physical makeup, and that the high-pitched conclusion, toward which all other events in the tale gradually build, is the denouement in the drama of his deteriorating mind.

More obviously and skillfully in "Usher" than in some of his other works, Poe centers on the house-as-mind symbolism and its ramifications. To the narrator, viewing the stone mansion is unnerving not just because of its evident decay (it is literally fissured and figuratively "cracked"), but because the mirror image of the mansion in the lake beside it shows how closely the house (as head) resembles his own reflection in the water. He does not directly tell us of this resemblance, as if he is reluctant to admit it to himself, much less to others. Mirror images are not exact reproductions of what they reflect, and so the off-center image in the water may terrify him all the more because it reflects/exposes his own chaotic mindset. Like many other Poe narrators, for example those in "MS. Found in a Bottle," "The Tell-Tale Heart," "The Black Cat" or "The Murders in the Rue Morgue," this storyteller tries to convince us of the validity in his narrative, though like others, too, he slips up every now and then, providing a key to his own unreliability. The Usher siblings are by no means the only "sick" characters in this narrative; the narrator seems similarly debilitated.

Just as interesting are the orchestrated departures from everyday life as he moves farther into the House of Usher (literally as he proceeds to Roderick's personal chamber, and figuratively as he delves into the depths of his own mind/self). The "singularly dreary tract of country" traversed by the narrator while he rides to the House of Usher provides a setting at once realistic and fantastic. This tract could exist anywhere, and here it becomes a splendid metaphor for the narrator-protagonist's own mind/self. Arrived at the House of Usher, he leaves his horse with a servant. Neither horse nor servant reappears. The doctor, who is departing as the narrator proceeds toward Roderick's chamber, also vanishes, and the servant who leads the narrator to Roderick is likewise seen no more. The three men met by the narrator, in addition to the horse, represent aspects of normalcy from which the narrator becomes increasingly distant. The horse, in Poe's era a creature of mundane utility but in folklore, as previously noted, a creature endowed with intelligence and strong sexual impulses, represents, in the context of "Usher," physical, tangible aspects potential in its master's life. Thus the narrator's approaching and entering the mansion signals his leaving an everyday world, even if that is bleak for him, for one where physical and emotional parts of life have become unbalanced, engendering increasingly unhappy and destructive consequences. The horse and the three humans who never reappear interact only briefly with the narrator: implicitly, reality is being left behind for a future that can lead only to misfortune.

Roderick is without doubt physically and (even more) mentally unstable, but his appeal to the narrator is strong. Their friendship stems from childhood, suggesting that Roderick plays some vital part in the narrator's life, as indeed proves to be the case – the narrator cannot leave before the house and its owners have thoroughly terrified him. Roderick states that his own major malady is fear of fear itself, and that he will perish because of fear. Fear of what, we might well ask? That answer is deferred, but the ravages of stress on Roderick's organic health are unmistakable. Meanwhile the narrator learns (for the first time, oddly enough, considering the longtime and close friendship between Usher and him), that Roderick has a twin sister who is apparently dying. Poe's diction regarding Madeline, who is "evidently approaching dissolution" (*M* 1: 403–4), is delightfully ambiguous, and for good artistic purpose, as we later comprehend. Significantly, too, as Usher speaks about Madeline, she passes through "a remote portion of the apartment, and, without having noticed my presence, disappeared" (*M* 1: 404).

If the narrator is witnessing a drama of psychosomatic implications playing out before him, and if that drama mimes his own emotional-physical state, his angst is understandable (to us, if not to him). He and Roderick represent artist figures, the narrator as storyteller, Roderick as poet, musician, painter. Wholly caught up in artistic/emotional concerns, neither gives equal energy to the earthiness that would contribute to their leading ordinary lives. In context, Roderick's burial of his sister, who is subject to cataleptic trances (what we today call epilepsy), symbolizes repression of an important element in life, namely the physical. That importance is borne out by Madeline's name, which has triple roots. First, "Madeline" derives from Mary Magdalene, and even though that biblical woman became saintly, legend credits her with being a prostitute before her redemption by Christ. Madeline's name also means "lady of the house," which Madeline Usher assuredly is, and "tower of strength." Because of Madeline's illness, this last connotation may seem ironic, although it is altogether appropriate and realistic, if subtly wrought by means of Poe's imaginative vision.

Seemingly digressing, I now point out the disparity between Madeline's debilitated appearance and her eventual feats of great physical strength. How could she escape from a sealed coffin? How could she open the door to her death chamber, a door so heavy and warped that even Roderick and the narrator could not move it without difficulty – albeit they may not be in prime physical condition? How can she then ascend from the sub-cellar to an upper floor to confront Roderick, which is another seemingly impossible feat for one so ill and weak, who has been left for dead? Even if Madeline was not dead but, as Roderick states, was placed "*living in the tomb!*" (*M* 2: 416), how has she managed this miraculous return? The answer is actually simple: Madeline is a vampire, or, rather, she is a vampire figure adroitly refashioned by Poe to symbolize psycho-physical forces that relate her to Roderick, to their house and to the narrator. Vampires exist in a state between life and death, so they are often called the undead. They are capable of surviving long spans of time without imbibing their ascribed nourishment, blood from live humans. During such intervals they may become quite emaciated in appearance, though they can quickly rebound with all their strength intact. Vampires are also credited with preying first on their family members and other loved ones, then moving out to widen the circle of their victims.

Previously, in order to soothe his friend, the narrator has elected to read to the invalid books, for which he supplies the titles, of special interest for Roderick. All but one treat interconnections between animal and vegetable life or, as Poe may have thought, between spirit and matter (*M* 2: 419 n15). The title of the book cited last is, translated from Latin, *Vigils for the Dead at the Second Church of Mainz* (1500).We may well ask what significance such a book would have in company with the others, and how Poe would have known about it. The second question may never be definitively answered, but the first is really more to the point for our purposes. In addition to its normal use, the *Vigiliae* was employed to ward off vampires. As a vampire figure Madeline would have had little trouble in freeing herself from the coffin and the burial chamber where she was kept to frustrate grave robbers. Her looking more alive after she is presumed dead is another vampire trait. Aware of his twin's condition, Roderick was reluctant to perform a ritual killing that would free her from vampire taint, was reluctant, too, to bury her in a remote cemetery, where grave robbers could exhume the corpse for medical purposes. Medical personnel would have understood the symptoms of vampirism and ended Madeline's vampire existence, so the family doctor's knowledge of his patient might have caused Roderick's reluctance to bury her in the open graveyard.

"Usher," then, is sophisticated literary art, in which Poe again uses folklore, along with his knowledge of medicine, to bolster the subtle but firm psychological underpinnings of this terror tale. Precise sources of Poe's knowledge of vampirism have not been documented, but his characterization of Madeline comports well with general vampire lore. If she and Roderick share a soul with their house (in all senses of that word), and they are all doomed because Roderick refuses to partake of the physical in life (thus debilitating all parts of this triad), Madeline may have turned vampire to immortalize herself whenever Roderick and the house should cease to exist. If she represents what Roderick fears and tries to "bury," her return as an appalling creature bent on revenge might have prompted Poe's creating her as an appalling vampire figure.

Additional possibilities relevant to Roderick's burial of Madeline return us to intimations in her name. The Mary Magdalene derivation may point to sexuality as a cause of trouble in the Usher house ("house" connoting the psycho-physical condition of the Ushers). Some readers believe that Roderick and Madeline committed incest, and that that act creates their tragedy. If incest were actual sexual intercourse – and the text nowhere supports that it was – we might see the tragic end of both Ushers as inevitable, given that incest in Romantic literature was always destructive. Whether or not actual incest was committed, Roderick may have harbored incest fantasies, but then wanted to "bury" them. The siblings' demise may also result because the sentient house, which imprisons them, takes umbrage at such impulses, finally destroying all involved. Although the third implication in Madeline's name, "tower of strength," most readily alludes to her escaping her tomb, it could encompass another possibility. Roderick's debilitation symbolizes the end of the Usher line because his overbalancing himself toward art diminishes sexual potency. In that respect, Madeline becomes a tower of strength in another way – vampirism has often been equated with rampant sex. Madeline displays the brute strength more commonly associated with males, so she may equate with phallicness, though such phallicness is unnatural and death-dealing, not life-promoting.

Like Ligeia and Morella, Madeline causes greater havoc in her male antago-nist's (Roderick's) emotions than she does on his body (unless, of course, she has preyed on him in the traditional vampire way, which victimization may have brought about his emaciation and weakness, as well as robbing him of any ability to create art that might be pleasantly inspiring instead of fright-ening). The narrator's witnessing the downfall of the Ushers dramatizes his own physical and emotional instability, so his succumbing to, then recoiling from, such an experience naturally makes for a tale of mystery and sensation. Since there are more male than female characters in "Usher," the entombing of Madeline while she still lives may signal Roderick's and his friend's retreat from realities in life, which encompass physical health and normal sexuality – as Poe's generation would have known it, i.e. heterosexuality. If we admit that this retreating is allegorically bound up in the narrative, then the men's inter-actions are understandably brief and tentative. In context, she first appears remote and shadowy as she crosses Roderick's apartment (symbolically, the center of uncomprehending or, maybe, guilt-ridden masculinity); later, in her coffin, she looks almost alive, and her return is presented as a fearsome and bloody being. These configurations are redolent of displacements of crucial elements of life, whence the rebound is terrifying.

If Madeline represents earth-physical life, which Roderick fears and tries to repress/deny, their final encounter plausibly depicts repression's violently bursting free. The blood on her person may mark her as a vampire of the mere entertainment stamp, but it may also symbolize the reality of life itself, which nobody escapes, and which concludes in death. As frequently as "house" resonates throughout this tale, we should not forget that blood may be syn-onymous with that term. The mere sight of Madeline accelerates Roderick's death – by fear more so than by a vampire's bite. As in many other vampire stories, Madeline's falling upon Roderick represents her claiming his will, and therefore his dying from fear, the stress of which can bring about death.

Can we wonder that the narrator flees before the final dissolution of the house(s) of Usher? Moreover, was the moon actually blood red, or was this sight another figment of the narrator's own crumbling psychosomatic stability, a stability that must not have been strong since it ultimately could not resist what he witnessed during his "sojourn of some weeks" in the "mansion of gloom" (*M* 2: 398). Poe's narrator bears kinship with many another literary character who decides to "sojourn," to repeat Poe's own term, within what are to him alien, or seemingly alien, conditions, nonetheless assuming that he will return to his better-known (status quo) way of life. Ironically, such protagonists learn either that entry into and experiencing such conditions may prove too foreign for their wellbeing, or that they really visit their own emotional depths, which prove to be frightening. As this protagonist remarks in the opening sections, though, he has "found him*self*" (emphasis mine) upon arrival at the House of Usher. Therefore his own perceptions of the house and what it represents might be subject to question (*M* 2: 397–98). What a house and what a self he ultimately experiences! "The Fall of the House of Usher" makes fine companion reading to works such as Hawthorne's "Young Goodman Brown" (1835), because Goodman Brown undertakes a similar sojourn, only to come to grief because he discovers too much about himself and others as they relate to his self. The converse, just to cite another example from Poe's contemporaries, may be seen in Henry Thoreau's *Walden* (1854). There the sojourner gains emotional vitality from his sojourn by Walden Pond. Many other works in American literature are focused upon protagonists who imagine that just once, and briefly, they can experiment with some unfamiliar aspect of life, then eschew it as if it had had no lasting effects upon them. Absent from this equation is, of course, any forethought that they may face the unpredictable, over which they have no control. Loss of control soon impinges on them, however, and gradually unhinges them. Long ago, Poe defined such loss as terror that originates in the soul. In "Usher," the narrator's glimpse into his own soul, which he shares with the Ushers and their house, overwhelms him – but affords him the makings of great fiction. For such dramas of the protagonist's collapse (in "Usher" and in many other works), Poe deftly employed and artistically modified the props and characters from antecedent Gothic tradition, extending it to create what are vignettes of the mind at war. In his tales and poems we confront what seem to be very modern situations, thereby making Poe's writings speak meaningfully to our own emotional lives.

One must not leave Poe's tales about women without referencing the last among them, "Eleonora" (1842). In an inversion of the emotional and physical horrors in the earlier tales with women's names, this one ends happily. Several critiques that premise biographical origins for "Eleonora" may have a measure of credibility, but Poe's art looms larger in other ways. Once again we encounter a heroine whose name devolves from the same stem as "Helen" and "Lenore," with all the implications of fostering balance and sanity in the self that we have seen in regard to those so named. In addition, "Eleonora" is cast into lyrical prose surpassing that in any other of the tales about women, though many such passages exist in those tales.

The narrator in the first version of "Eleonora" (1841) gave "Pyrros" as his name, thereby recalling the ancient philosopher who disbelieved in certainty (*M* 2: 645). Doubtfulness would be in keeping with the narrator's confusion during much of "Eleonora," as well as with readers' wonder concerning the conclusion: was the blessing mentioned by the narrator after his second marriage the voice of Eleonora (from the spirit world) or a figment of his imagination? That the first version of the tale was entitled "Eleonora. A Fable" compounds ambiguities, as does the narrator's brief disquisition about madness (a topic elsewhere used by Poe and obviously of great interest to him). The subtitle and a name for the narrator were eliminated in revision, strengthening psychological universality in the tale.

The union of the narrator and Eleonora plausibly represents youthful passion in an idyllic rural setting redolent of the innocence of inexperience in life. Eleonora's death and her bereaved lover's removal to urban environs may in context indicate his increasing maturity, in which young love played a crucial role, but from which he had to move on to a more matured, balanced state of being. Although his marriage to Ermengarde is not without passion, its association with the peaceful sleep invoked by the shade of Eleonora negates any curse that had been invested in their early, seemingly indissoluble, bonding. The ensuing pleasant union with Ermengarde was foreshadowed by a motto, which Mabbott translates as "Under the protection of a specific form the soul is safe" (*M* 2: 645). Soul, we must remember, is often synonymous with "psyche," or the mind. Since that term derives from the Psyche of Classical mythology, who nurtured love or the emotional element in life and the self, Poe's context is understandable. Ermengarde provides the form that restores balance/beauty to the narrator's being. Noteworthy, too, by way of contrasts, is the narrator's phrase, "I found myself" (*M* 2: 644), once he gains his later, urban location. Here, this comment is positive; conversely, the narrator in an earlier tale tells us that "I . . . found myself, as the shades of the evening drew on, within view

of the melancholy House of Usher" (*M* 2: 397). Finding one's self is a preoccupation with many Poe narrators, and one that buttresses interpreting many
works by Poe as oriented toward subtly psychological fiction, which surpasses
the quality of the cheap-thrill variety of Gothic tales.

More often than not, "Eleonora" has been omitted from critiques of Poe's
tales about women (as has "The Assignation"); consequently a slanted view
of Poe's own attitude toward women has been read into these tales. Grim and
gruesome though the earlier tales about women may have been, the negative
context results from the male protagonist's distorting or unbalancing what
should be a harmonious union. Because of recent psychological hypotheses –
that each of us, no matter our external appearance or apparent emotional
outreach, is composed of far greater minglings of masculinity and femininity
than long tradition has credited – Poe must be seen as light years ahead of his
time in his perceptions of such interminglings. Therefore the happy ending in
"Eleonora" foregrounds, more emphatically than most of the earlier women
tales, balances in gender as essential to a healthy self. This last of Poe's tales
about women suggests that Poe's imaginative vision has developed/matured,
and so its outreach is far less terrifyingly Gothic than that in its predecessors.
The Valley of the Many-Colored Grass is Edenic, of course, but the urban setting
to which the narrator eventually removes resonates no depressing aftermath of
the expulsion from Eden. Nor does it suggest anything else that is negative. The
greater lyricism in form (rhymed prose in certain passages) strengthens the
positive note in the conclusion of "Eleonora." One might conclude, too, that,
as in much else in life, bad news seems to stimulate greater interest than good
news does, and so the greater length in the earlier women tales exemplifies that
predisposition.

Many of Poe's other tales do not cluster like those in which beautiful dying or
dead women are central, though this heterogeneity should in no way make us
think that these other tales lack literary art. For example, just about every tale
by Poe features as narrator a flaneur. Strictly, a flaneur is defined as an "aimless
person," though the secondary definition, "a man about town," has come to
have greater currency in literary contexts. Poe's narrators are often far from
aimless, because they hope to convince other characters, as well as readers, that
what they are relating to us are straightforward accounts of events – and in the
majority of Poe's tales (and poems) the events are sensational.

Several of the narrators in tales already mentioned seem to be telling one
story, only to commit Freudian slips that alert us to another story embedded
within the first. "The Assignation," "The Fall of the House of Usher" and "The
Cask of Amontillado" number among such works, but additional excellent
examples may be found, for example in "The Pit and the Pendulum" (1842),

"The Black Cat" (1843) and "The Tell-Tale Heart" (1843). In these, and in many others among Poe's tales and poems, what the narrators try unsuccessfully to conceal is that the story really revolves around their individual concerns much more than those of other characters or situations they try to present as the crucial center in their narrative(s).

Of course, in "The Pit and the Pendulum" the narrator is positioned front and center throughout, with any other character being either absent or only minimally glimpsed (one of his persecutors) or mentioned (his rescuer). The results of what the other characters do to the narrator's state of being are fore-grounded, not that the narrator's physical interactions with others are detailed. Poe cleverly manipulates conventions of terror-tale situations (Inquisition victims condemned to terrifying imprisonment and isolation, their psychological traumas intensified by possibilities of physical tortures and accentuated by the eerie, frightening pit, the razor-edged pendulum and the heated metal walls) to achieve a tale of the narrator's journey into the depths of his own self, which descent does not reveal to him much that is heartening. The narrator is confused about his relationship with time, represented by the pendulum, and the void, symbolized by the pit. Obviously, the major concern that has led to his imprisonment is some genuine or trumped up moral issue, which his examiners consider criminal. His rescue stands as a respite from the acutely frightening terrors that time and the void may bring to one. Thus "The Pit and the Pendulum" makes companion reading for "The Masque of the Red Death" where the paranoias of Prospero and his followers, who represent irrational fantasies about evading time (and that for which time is an inescapable reality: life), bring tragedy to those who desire to escape life's realities, symbolized by the clock and blood. Readers may, however, view the progression of time toward death as a wholly normal aspect of life. The difference between Poe's two tales is that the narrator in "The Pit and the Pendulum" gains a reprieve, as the characters in "Masque" do not. Interestingly, in both tales weird lighting intermittently illuminates a scene with glaring effects, enhancing the disturbed minds of the revelers in "Masque" and of the narrator in "The Pit and the Pendulum." The fiery lighting created when the walls are heated in the latter tale may be mirrors of the overstrained emotions roused in the hapless prisoner as he watches the walls change and comments on the torturing effects as those hot movable panels close in upon him. This is one of the few Poe tales in which a downward spiral journey is reversed so the protagonist is delivered from literally and figuratively going over the edge, "A Descent into the Maelström" being another. Both tales are precise renderings of powerful psychological states, which bear out Poe's dictum that, in his fiction, terror emanates from the human mind.

"The Black Cat" and "The Tell-Tale Heart" also stand as companion pieces in which terrors well up in the mind(s) of the narrator(s). In the former, the narrator's insistence that his reactions to pets are implicated in his murder of his wife – and walling up her corpse in the cellar – is suspect, to say the least. His thoughts and actions have belied this rationalization, and the ultimate revelation of the truth suggests that he himself has not really believed unquestionably in such would-be justifications. Effects of alcohol may contribute no mean share to his murderous impulses, making the tale one in which alcohol has no connection with comedy. Because sharply divided attitudes toward alcohol consumption were timely issues in Poe's day, he may in part have calculated on appealing to temperance advocates (i.e. people who were anti-alcohol).[11] The narrator's intense relationships with the cats may exemplify a reversal of the usual animal-as-beastly/human-as-rational paradigm. Ironically the cats seem to harbor far more genuine humaneness than their master does, and in the end the narrator's brutality and its results seem to prompt him to spontaneous confession. The live burial motif may deepen the narrator's repressed emotions, but such repression cannot be long sustained without leading to explosive reactions, precisely the case in "The Black Cat." Since in folklore black cats are unpredictable, but usually evil creatures, the discovery of the murder because of the cat's cries adds another irony to this tale.

Much more brief, "The Tell-Tale Heart" repeats the situation of foul murder, though here we confront premeditated murder of an old man by the narrator, who may very likely be his caregiver. As in "The Black Cat," the more strenuously the narrator tries to convince us of his sanity, the more he convinces us that he is deranged. Here is another tale of cruelty to the living old man and brutality to his corpse. Foolishly, the murderer buries the body parts under the steps, inviting the police, who arrive at neighbors' request, to position themselves near the burial place. All the while the narrator's guilty conscience, his "heart," has seemed to throb relentlessly to him alone, causing him finally to blurt out that he has murdered the old man. Along with the storyteller in "The Black Cat," this narrator is impelled to confession, all previous bragging to the contrary going for naught. The greater brevity in "The Tell-Tale Heart" is in perfect keeping with the mounting intensity of the narrator's emotions, which rapidly increase to the breaking point. In these two tales, as is so typical of Poe's characters, the protagonists' murders may represent their killing, or attempting to repress, key elements in what should be a balanced self. The imbalancings are eventually self-destructive, and, it should be emphasized, such destruction often requires no great time to take effect.

With so many works about sanity versus madness to his credit, is it any wonder that Poe should create a tale like "The System of Dr. Tarr and Professor

Fether"? The deliberate blurring between sanity and insanity, in a madhouse setting no less, is excellent technique. The reversed situations, in which the madmen temporarily overpower and lock up their keepers, are not revealed until the boisterous conclusion of the tale, but meantime the oh-so-earnest, but oh-so-imperceptive narrator unwittingly inspires us to uncertainties regarding the actions he witnesses among the others, all the while missing the signifi-cance of these events himself. Treatment of mental illness in Poe's era was just emerging from primitive methods, so he naturally became interested in this timely topic. He was, however, not sympathetic to what he considered the caretakers' too heedlessly trusting their patients, as "Tarr and Fether" suggests in a way that correlates with Poe's distrust of democracy – which, he thought, would lead to mob rule.

Some argue that Poe's real intent in this tale (and several others) was to devise coded alarms concerning untrustworthy conduct among African-American slaves, with hints of uprisings in which reprisals toward slave owners would lead to horrendous atrocities. One begins to wonder, though, whenever a monkey or ape appears in antebellum American literature, if that animal represents an image dear to racists, of a volatile African-American. In light of Poe's own comic impulses, I find greater plausibility in reading "Tarr and Fether" as parodic, the targets being Poe's own earlier tales, "The Fall of the House of Usher," "The Masque of the Red Death" and the Dupin tales, mainly "The Murders in the Rue Morgue" (because of its hints of Dupin's madness, which prove in the end to be groundless, and because of the unpredictable orang-utan). The apelike characters in "Tarr and Fether" – apelike because they have literally been tarred and feathered in a reflection of the punishment meted out to many criminals – seem to have far less certain associations with racial issues than they do with Poe's own literary creations. This same principle holds true for "Hop-Frog," where the oppression of the dwarfish court jester and his companion, Tripetta, offers just as much credence for alcoholism as for racism in this later tale.[12]

## The novels and *Eureka*

For many years, Poe's experiments in novel writing were dismissed as testimony to his real accomplishments residing in the lyric poem and the short story, or "tale" as he preferred. Reviewers of Poe's first novel, *The Narrative of Arthur Gordon Pym* (1838), were quick to comment on realistic and hoax features, but other opinions, especially those from academic critics from the mid-twentieth century forward, rank the novel as one of Poe's most significant achievements, if one that is not entirely forthright in meaning. Poe himself remarked several years after the publication of *Pym* that the novel was a "very silly book," though because his remark was part of a letter criticizing William E. Burton, who was dismissing Poe from *Burton's Gentleman's Magazine*, we might disregard Poe's deprecation as being his final opinion of *Pym* (*O*: 130). He certainly was not reluctant elsewhere to mention the novel as a worthwhile accomplishment whenever such citations might benefit him, creating thereby another enigma.

Poe's abortive attempts to publish "Tales of the Folio Club" finally led James Kirke Paulding (an older, long-established American author whose help Poe had enlisted to promote publication of his book, and who wrote to White and to Poe after Harpers rejected the manuscript because they felt that Poe's humor was too subtle) to respond that Poe should put his fine artistic abilities to work on a novel that would lampoon the "faults and foibles of our own people, their peculiarities of habits and manners, and above all the ridiculous affections and extravagancies of fashionable English literature of the day which we copy with admirable success and servility."[13] Poe heeded the older author's advice, producing what we might categorize as a notably American book, though he applied his own methods in carrying out that advice in *Pym*. He serialized the opening portions in the January and February 1837 issues of the *Southern Literary Messenger*; the full-length novel (with those early installments revised somewhat) appeared from Harpers, 30 July 1838.

Like Herman Melville's *Moby-Dick* (1851), for which *Pym* was a partial inspiration, Poe's novel features American enterprise on the ocean, but whereas Melville centered his novel in the whaling industry, Poe focused his on scientific exploration into Antarctic regions. These territories had not been explored to any great extent, so to Poe's readers during the 1830s they savored of the unknown and mysterious. The South Pole, like its northern counterpart, held out interest as a possible entrance into the earth's core, and the "holes at the poles" theory was at that time an intriguing topic. In their respective novels Poe and Melville showed awareness about elements of (often sensational) adventure as well as the tedious routines that were parts of sailors' lives. Overall, though, *Pym* is far more lurid than *Moby-Dick*. Both may be classified as novels of adventure at sea, but the nature of adventure in both has far greater subtleties than are customary in popular nineteenth-century action-centered tales of oceanic adventure which, for the most part, lack subtle psychological depth, for example the sea fictions of Sir Walter Scott, Frederick Marryat or James Fenimore Cooper. *Pym* and *Moby-Dick* also hint strongly at the difficulties in desiring exclusive meaning from a literary text.

The narrative proper in *Pym* commences with episodes common in nineteenth-century boys' adventure stories. Arthur Gordon Pym and his friend, Augustus Barnard, set out to lark in a small boat, the *Ariel*. That craft is soon destroyed as a larger craft, the *Penguin*, overrides it; Pym sustains a neck injury of mortal proportions, but from which he speedily recovers – all too speedily and completely, it would seem, thus introducing a miraculous, or satiric, note: is Pym's recovery a genuine rapid healing or is this episode, which invites us to think "tall tale," more significant as a taxing of our credibility, thus contributing to the comic thrusts in the novel? As in other tales of adventure, initiation, maturing, *Pym* presents a journey into life by the protagonist, here centered in Pym's voyaging far south from his native Nantucket. Once he leaves the settled and civilized world, disturbing but educating events move him from a halcyon boyhood toward a greater maturity.

In the "Preface" to *Pym*, Poe strongly insinuates that readers might carefully heed shifts from appearance to reality within the text because such alternations and deceptions confuse one's perceptions. He states that Pym's manuscript came into his hands for editing, so he chose to present it in the guise of fiction. This technique further obscures distinctions between appearance and reality or fact and fiction. Overall, the "Preface" establishes a satiric lead-in to the narrative. The precise nature, if there is a precise nature, of Poe's satire draws varied responses, which have encouraged controversies regarding *Pym*. Such bewildering transitions as Pym endures continue throughout the novel, during which Pym and his new friend, Dirk Peters, elude the worst effects brought about amidst adventures punctuated by atrocities on the seas and on Tsalal, the southern land they eventually explore.

On Tsalal they encountered ambiguous and at times near death-dealing interactions with the inhabitants. Escaping to the sea in a canoe, taking with them a Tsalalian, Nu-Nu, they sail into mysterious warm waters, which Pym appropriately terms a "region of novelty and wonder." An unsettling mistiness now envelops them, white ashy particles begin to fall like rain, and weird animals pass by their canoe. Nu-Nu, who can explain none of these eerie phenomena, eventually dies, lying in the bottom of the canoe. An ever more rapid current now propels them uncontrollably, moving them directly toward a giant white figure who will engulf them. A brief postscript relates something of the outcome for the characters, though once again what is related smacks of deception, and so, with ambiguities being paramount, the text closes much as it began.

The foregoing synopsis hardly does justice to the subtleties interwoven into the texture of *Pym*. Is it a bungled work which was broken off because Poe could not fathom how to continue (what he should probably not have begun, i.e. a long work of fiction instead of a short story); does it join other works that have been designated Romantic fragments (as if they constitute a recognizable genre); or is it indeed a thematically and structurally sound whole? If it is complete, what does/may it convey to readers? What about hoax versus plausibility? Essentially this novel sets forth Pym's progression through physical and emotional changes and disturbances that are likely to mature him, as I remarked above. The maturing process requires Pym's negotiating many experiences that force him to examine and question his outlook. These experiences bring him into contact with others whose influences further his development. Combined, these situations convey (to readers, if not to Pym) greater awareness of how first impressions may be woefully inaccurate – what we usually think of as parts of the maturing process. Such realizations often shatter Pym's perceptions, just as they serve to maintain reader interest.

The live burial motifs (when the *Penguin* overruns the *Ariel*, when Pym is confined to the hold of the *Grampus*, when Pym and Peters nearly perish under tons of earth loosened with murderous intent by the Tsalalians) may represent stages of growth for Pym, who luckily resurrects, we might say, from each, with his awareness shaken and expanded, whether he consciously registers that fact or not. So those live burial episodes – that have often been castigated by unsympathetic readers as evidence of Poe's charnel-house imagination at work – function symbolically to enhance psychological plausibility in the novel. The occurrences themselves may be sensational, but they contribute to the reality of a character's journeying through increasingly fantastic, though not any less unreal, circumstances.

The voyaging and other exploration are deft metaphors for Pym's moving from the known and familiar into strange geographical regions and to below-surface emotional depths within his self. So *Pym* resembles Poe's poems and tales about journeying into the self. Introspective as he is, Pym takes a voyage of discovery onto strange seas of thought indeed. Not for nothing do such phrases as "finding myself" "I found myself" and the like pepper the pages in this book. Departing land to voyage adventurously on water may be a boyhood fantasy, but it may also represent one's engaging what is often deemed the greatest source of all life, i.e. water, which has impressive (and, in context, symbolic) deeps to plumb as one quests after unfamiliar, generally non-rational aspects of life. This questing contributes to the psychological substance in Poe's novel.

As he composed *Pym*, Poe's creative imagination took his protagonist more and more intensely into emotional adventure, often symbolized by his surroundings, as Melville did in composing *Moby-Dick* or Mark Twain in transforming what commenced as a boy's action-adventure story to a more subtly symbolic fiction, especially in the sections centered in Huck's travels on the river, in *Adventures of Huckleberry Finn* (1885). Of interest, too, one wonders whether Twain may have read *Pym* because many of Huck's fantasies abound in catastrophes revolving around persons' calamities, violence and death. Many subsequent American (and other) literary works have followed such patterns in taking their protagonists to levels of maturity they had not possessed when they were introduced. A similar operative principle underlies another work from Poe's own era, H. D. Thoreau's *Walden* (1854): that one is drawn to water in order to foster imaginative awareness and liberation, all in the name of self-realization. One could look ahead many years to "The Lake Isle of Innisfree" (1893), that magnificent poem by William Butler Yeats, where like sentiments prevail.

Pym moves from a locale of relatively mundane reality (Nantucket, Pym's father's occupation, boys' experimenting with alcohol and what ensues, an accident on the water, Pym's deceiving his grandfather) into ever greater fantasy surroundings (the eerie southern regions and strange people found there, culminating in the giant weird figure in the awesome conclusion). His "voyaging" leads him into greater geographical exploration, to circumstances beyond what are customary to him in regard to his immediate physical wants (e.g. hunger, thirst), to friendship and trust, to sexuality, to subjective and broader issues of identity – all of which seem to involve surprises natural in one's maturing beyond sheltered childhood.

The narrative proper commences with Pym's giving us his name, or naming himself, paralleling the narrator's method of identifying himself in "William Wilson" or in the first version of "Eleonora," and that of Melville's Ishmael in *Moby-Dick*. For these characters, naming emphasizes the issue of identity, and that issue continues to be crucial throughout Pym's account. Many more passages in *Pym* involve significant names – of characters and of other important subject matter – which attest Poe's literary art. For example, to some readers Pym's name resonates with that of Poe's own triple name. We should remember, though, that Poe seldom used the Allan part of his name, more often signing as Edgar A. Poe. Therefore Arthur Gordon Pym represents no guarantee that Poe's name or Poe the man is reflected within the text of *Pym*, though some critics contend zealously that autobiographical materials are important in the book.

More persuasive, "Pym" may be an anagram for "imp" (*P* 1: 217), and an impishness does seem to permeate much of Poe's novel. Since we repeatedly encountered suggestions of the act of writing itself, as well as the language that goes into written work (editing, turning Pym's account into fictional form, Augustus' written communication with Pym, the strange letters and the comment about them in the "Note"), and since Poe elsewhere had a bit of fun, whatever other purposes he may have had, in his pronouncements about writing (which I will address in the section on Poe's criticism), such impishness is altogether plausible. To digress briefly, but not unwittingly, I cite as examples of Pym's own impishness his tomfoolery when meeting his grandfather, Augustus' response when Pym balks at his friend's plans for a midnight sailing, and Pym's later masquerading aboard ship as a corpse. We might also understandably recall in context here the impish uses of names in "The Assignation," "Bon-Bon" and "The Murders in the Rue Morgue." Respectively the wordplay in Thomas Moore–Thomas More, in Pierre Bon-Bon, and in Dupin–duping, plus the police's primary suspect being a man whose name means "the good": all these examples, and many more, exist in the Poe canon, reinforcing the idea that impishness underlies Pym's name.

Pym's childhood friend Augustus may represent the order and balance that typify the Neoclassicism in eighteenth- and early nineteenth-century Anglo-American culture, though some of the scrapes that come to him and Pym may lead us to wonder about reason and balance. Interestingly, the character Augustus Scratchaway in the Folio Club may suffer a fate similar to Augustus Barnard's, i.e. each is left behind as the mainspring character who temporarily associates with them moves on to more Romantic aspects of life. Augustus' note to Pym in the hold might be a "scratching away," which would serve as a link between the Folio Club and *Pym*. If Augustus Barnard is introduced as a mildly comic character, his revolting lingering death diminishes any good humor that lurks in his name. That same trajectory operates in his enticing Pym to undertake some wild adventuring, but once the voyaging (literal and metaphoric) proceeds what Augustus represents no longer contributes significantly to Pym's development, and so his influence becomes inessential.

Additional wordplay resides in the naming of Pym's home town Edgarton. Not only does that offer a colloquial pronunciation of Edgartown, but it reminds us that the actual town is not on Nantucket, but on the neighboring island, Martha's Vineyard. In light of the motifs of food and drink in *Pym*, added to which are several important scenes in which drunkenness is crucial, one may understandably wonder if there is a comic impulse lurking within the text to test readers' attentiveness to places and what their names may insinuate – in this case the deliberate, if inverted, calling attention to vineyard for its connection with drinking and intoxication. Such testing continues, for readers and, understandably, for Pym. Poe indeed may have adapted techniques and themes associated with food and drink from "Tales of the Folio Club" when he composed *Pym*.[14]

To return more directly to characters' names (and there is purpose in those names), I cite several which in a cursory reading might not seem important, but which should not be ignored. Toward the end of chapter 6, for example, we find among the crew members on the *Grampus* who seem to be alien to the causes of Pym and Peters one Simms, who because he was drunk fell overboard and drowned, plus Greely and William Allen, these names perhaps satiric hits at William Gilmore Simms, an important antebellum Southern writer whose work Poe knew, Horace Greeley, a prominent New York editor who had acclaimed Poe's critiques in the *Southern Literary Messenger*, and John Allan, Poe's late foster father, who, Poe felt, had treated him unjustly. Their drinking and boisterousness heighten the satire upon renowned men, several prominent in the American literary world, appearing in bad straits. One might also detect Poe's more serious predilections for psychologically oriented literature in two other names, William and Wilson, which resonate of the human will, which mental faculty seemed to be a preoccupation with Poe, witness "Ligeia," "William Wilson" and "The Fall of the House of Usher." Less obtrusive but nonetheless significant, human will is the major operative in "The Cask of Amontillado," "Hop-Frog" and poems such as "The Raven" and "Ulalume," though one might also recall "Metzengerstein" in this context.

Not all the names are, however, comic in intent. Comic or grave, Poe's namings should not be lightly passed over in *Pym* (or elsewhere in the Poe canon, as I have suggested). Pym's own first name, Arthur, may at once categorize him as a hero, as any other literary character so named may be reminiscent of the legendary King Arthur. That Arthur is not entirely without blemish, as some versions of the legendry depict him. He may have been an illegitimate child, and he may have committed incest. He also seems to have been sexually inadequate in his own marriage, thus precipitating his queen's affair with Lancelot, his favorite knight, and illicit sex is key in the breakup of the Round Table. Since sexual issues swirl around this legendary figure, it may be no surprise that sexual implications form one important undercurrent relevant to Poe's Arthur Pym. Pym is in many respects no heroic hero. He is a less elevated figure, at least as regards royal attributes, and as a more humble protagonist he adumbrates long lines of heroes in American and other literary works.

Far more important in Pym's life journey is Dirk Peters, whose name "speaks volumes," to use a colloquialism that is apt in context here. Mentioned in rather derogatory terms in the "Preface," Peters quickly comes to assume major importance, once we engage the narrative text proper, as he and Pym establish a solid friendship. The male name "Dirk," of Teutonic origin, means "ruler of the people."[15] That origin is entirely fitting for Dirk Peters, whose canniness in regard to other persons and life in general is keenly penetrating. "Dirk" is also a colloquialism for a straight-blade, long dagger. The Peters part of his name, in tandem with his relationship to Pym, marks him out as Pym's guardian angel or savior on many occasions, thereby imparting to him a resemblance to

St. Peter, who may admit some to Heaven and send others toward the path to Hell. Peters's names form an interesting blending of salvation on the one hand, and ambiguities related to human sexuality (the dagger part of his name suggesting phallicness) on the other. His several rescues of Pym give him an important role in the novel. That he is something of a voluptuary, as he reveals in chapters 4 and 6, makes him an older role model for Pym's own developing sexuality, and Peters seems to be decidedly heterosexual in his desires. His partaking somewhat of animal traits of great strength and unpredictable nature also highlights qualities that may be acquirements necessary for Pym's moving beyond a reasonably carefree youth, which has about it an innocence that is shed as one moves toward and into adulthood.

Peters may exemplify one of Poe's recyclings, here of a character in Poe's earlier tale, "Bon-Bon," a restaurateur who plays a comic St. Peter to an equally comic Satan. The contest between St. Peter and the devil concerns souls, and in this tale – part of the Folio Club in its motifs of food and drink – the cream of the jest involves who will win the soul of Pierre Bon-Bon (i.e. the good Peter), though perhaps it should be written "sole," i.e. a variety of fish that is considered choice food. Pierre defeats the devil's plans to ensnare him, but the give and take have gourmandizing and intoxication as backdrop to heighten the comedy between the contending pair. Dirk Peters seems to be divorced from the good-humored comedy in the earlier tale, and he needs no alcohol to stimulate him. In fashioning Peters, Poe demonstrates that he could take what had been humorous characterization and rework it into greater symbolic depth. Moreover, Pierre Bon-Bon was no White–Indian half-breed. This mixture mates with Peters's proactive role in Pym's life to suggest that the latter may, in departing his home background, be willing to extend himself to persons of another race, perhaps emotionally projecting his outlook far beyond such provincialism, i.e. a reluctance to interact coequally with a person of another race or of mixed-race parentage. Just as significant, Pym leaves his maternal grandfather – wealthy Mr. Peterson, who will, however, remorselessly disinherit any potential heir who offends him – for a world where such wealth is meaningless. Instead of being a Peters's son Arthur becomes a friend of Dirk Peters, who seems to be wholly indifferent to class and wealth, and who functions well outside of civilization. Dirk's instinctive mode of being appeals to Pym because it constitutes discovery and education for him.

Poe may also have been writing half-banteringly (and, in other passages, quite seriously in creating this novel where everything seems to have a counterpart that must be noticed) when he turned to naming the sailing vessels. He could have known of the wreck of a Norfolk vessel named the *Ariel*, though he may also have thought of the boat that carried the English poet Shelley to his death. The ship that runs down Pym and Augustus, the *Penguin*, prepares the way for the penguins that appear later in the novel. Those birds seem to mimic human traits and actions, which often evince a pretentiousness not indigenous to the birds themselves. Then, too, the *Ariel* may recall the sprite in Shakespeare's *The Tempest*. Ariel does not leave the enchanted island of Setebos for the real world, as the others do. In *Pym* such enchantments as sprites perform give way before the more horrifying, realistic events that befall later, and that to Pym seem at times to have supernatural origins. His transfer from the *Ariel* to the *Penguin* may also signal a move toward greater exposure to animal or non-rational (but nevertheless realistic) elements in life and self. Those elements serve as a prelude to even more unpredictable circumstances as Pym journeys farther from civilization and into the unknown. Pym's next craft, the *Grampus*, is named for any of several whale species that is larger, stronger and potentially more dangerous than a penguin. What transpires on this ship takes Pym much more toward an animalistic, savage state that is far more brutal than his existence had been when the *Ariel* seemed to influence his destiny. The callousness and butchery he witnesses certainly resemble nothing from his life in Edgarton.

The next ship, and the last vessel given a name, that rescues Pym and Peters, the *Jane Guy*, is also tellingly named. Jane, a feminine name, may contribute a latitude in gender issues in *Pym*. This ship functions as a potentially feminizing, nurturing presence, which would add breadth to Pym's initiation into life and self-realization. The "Guy" part of the name undercuts such breadth, however, because it may be a man's name or, as a verb, a term of deceit. Although this ship takes Pym to the island of Tsalal, where deception reaches a zenith in negative results, the ship and the Tsalalians who would destroy it are blown up, implying that Tsalal is unsympathetic to women or to the feminine presence, and that such unsympatheticness produces disaster. Since this island is located in far southern regions it may equate with Pym's geographical and psychological descent into vast depths in self that he never before had divined. Those depths are testing grounds for his own strength of self, what with seesawings between appearance and reality, between seeming friendship and actual savagery. The fire and explosion that destroy the *Jane Guy* may symbolize the Tsalalians' brute repression or "murder" of femininity, though that destruction rebounds when the explosion kills or horribly maims thousands of Tsalalians. The antagonism to femininity rebounds upon the predatory Tsalalians, who are "guyed" into supposing that they can destroy the ship, but who suffer dire consequences from what registers as fit retribution upon them.

The Tsalalians' skin is black, perhaps casting them as devil figures (the devil in folklore is often black), and their acts bolster such folklore linkages. Their blackness furnishes no absolute basis that they represent African-American slaves inflamed to revolt, as one line of approach, from the mid twentieth century forward, has contended. Poe's raven is black, too (the norm for his species), but that color makes him no more a figure of African-Americanness than is the orang-utan in "The Murders in the Rue Morgue": after all, orang-utans have reddish hair, no black coloring. Were there racial paranoias, specifically those about African-Americans, encoded within *Pym*, Poe's contemporaries, who were well aware of such fears, would surely have said so. No reviewer even hinted that possibility, however, nor were racial characteristics imputed to the apelike characters in "The System of Dr. Tarr and Professor Fether" or "Hop-Frog," which have been likened to African-Americans by some critics.

Rather than a dominant racial presence in *Pym*, that of the feminine, as I have suggested, seems more likely because interacting with the feminine would be significant in Pym's development from child to adult. He and Peters capture the Tsalalian, Nu-Nu, then escape in a canoe. Their flight takes them into fantastic waters, and they are finally caught up in a strong current that bears them directly into a merger with a weird giant white figure, who may plausibly symbolize a feminine presence; Pym's merging with femininity, astounding though that merger may be, marks the integration of masculinity with femininity, creating a balanced, integrated self. Other interpretations of the eerie white figure exist, but the feminine presence seems more plausible in context of Pym's self-discovery than do most other hypotheses, which range from autobiographical to religious significance in the figure.[16]

Fittingly, the novel ends because Pym's quest for self-realization has been achieved. Conversely, Nu-Nu, representative of Tsalalian outlook, dies because his existence is lopsided in giving scant heed to a feminine presence. Unlike Pym and Peters, the Tsalalians are prone to close ranks against any foreign being or thought, and so Nu-Nu's death reinforces the initiation theme in which such self-containment is destructive. The inevitable merging with the giant white figure as *Pym* concludes may incline one to think of this scene as Pym's merging with the feminine presence that this figure represents. A balancing of masculinity and femininity produces a unity. In Poe's creative writings, disaster results when such integration does not occur.

The ending of *Pym* in one respect resembles a technique more commonly found in another literary form, a technique that has attained cliché status. Traditionally, stage comedies end with mergings that represent the promoting of life, a point often reinforced by the performers forming a circle or simply joining hands while they stand in a straight line. Frequently, stage comedies feature courtship and marriage as plot staples, the courting providing the interest for the audience, and the marriage, or surety that marriage will take place between the central couple or couples, thus continuing/promoting life.

Just as significant, Pym stands out as a notably American literary protagonist because throughout the surface plot in the novel he remains essentially a loner. After all, he tells the story; he may be said to define the other characters for us; he eschews the known and routine in domestic life for that of travel-adventure-mystery. He is rootless, and his voyaging parallels the mobility of his contemporaries on land. Even though he is befriended by a stalwart like Peters, Pym retains, consciously or not, a kind of invisible yet firm barrier. His being the storyteller places him in a power position: is his account reliable? (We learn early on that it will be rife with the marvelous.) And if it is or is not, is either of those conditions a deliberate bit of sly deception of his audience, or is his account one of Naturalistic proportions, in which individuals are the pawns of uncontrollable forces? In other words does Pym-as-storyteller give us a trustworthy narrative, or is he a storyteller in the colloquial sense of that term, i.e. a liar or a trickster? Or have the consequences of his travels so worked upon his emotions that his inability to distinguish truth from fiction cautions us not to expect clarity in his narrative?

According to literary traditions of not going beyond a certain stage in the protagonists' lives, I believe that *Pym* ends (and artistically ends) with a male–female union, which signifies Pym's attaining a level of maturity beyond which we need not follow him. This technique emanates from Poe's own creative sense of such circumstances, and therefore the book is complete, not a failure of Poe's that had to be clumsily broken off because he could think of no more to add to the book. True, this novel is short in comparison with many other early nineteenth-century novels, but in that respect it approaches Poe's own critical precept that to be effective a work of genuine literary art must be brief.

My discussion of *Pym* merely hints at the multiplicity it holds out. I have already mentioned that every part seems to have a counterpart, so I add another example of this dualism. If in the "Preface" readers comprehend that deception will be a major feature in what follows, they will not be disappointed with Poe's techniques in deception. Despite any hoaxing – such as his wholesale pilfering of travel-exploration accounts (and that from one who warred in print against those whom he charged with plagiarism) – serious characterization is unmistakable, especially that of Pym and Peters. Poe's creation of a gradual transformation from an everyday into a fantastic world is equally outstanding. His modifying the conventional boys' adventure story into a richly textured symbolic novel likewise attests his creative genius. So *Pym* is not a work that Poe should not have undertaken because of any artistic deficiencies on his part.

Ironically, one reading of *Pym* may make a reader believe that no more repetitious, therefore absolutely deadly, piece of prose fiction exists. Read again, *Pym* may convince us to think that those very repetitions produce a hypnotic effect, which is appropriate expression of Pym's own drifting into a strange dreamlike world and as regards an author's drawing readers into the text. Recalling Samuel Taylor Coleridge's precept about the willing suspension of disbelief as one engages a literary text, we might think of Poe the poet literally trying to enchant us into his book, or, in other words, employing repetitions that constitute the means of singing readers into the text (the same process as enchanting in the verb sense of that word). I conclude as I began: *Pym* offers nothing if it does not continue to evade any single meaning, although each reader seems to have a particularly favorite theory about the book.[17]

Poe's second experiment in novel writing, *The Journal of Julius Rodman*, serialized in *Burton's Gentleman's Magazine*, January–June 1840, is far less sophisticated than *Pym*. A narrative about exploration of the western part of the North American continent (not yet then part of the USA), *Rodman* was calculated as timely fare for American readers, but it lacks the art found in *Pym*, and that it foundered is no wonder. Poe and Burton differed more and more over management of the magazine, concluding when Burton fired Poe. Those disturbances would surely have interfered with Poe's creative abilities, and he wrote no more novels. The technique in *Rodman* resembles the diary-entry forms found in "MS. Found in a Bottle," *Pym* and "The Lighthouse," Poe's unfinished tale, but the narrative flags because Poe drew so substantially from travel accounts about western exploration without contributing narrative coherence to those materials. As in *Pym*, several episodes of seeming violence (Rodman's party's meeting with Indians) and actual violence occur (the final installment features a nasty encounter with bears).

Rodman aligns with the characters in many Romantic poems of the Wordsworth school. He is introduced as a hypochondriac, so Nature intermittently seems bleak to him, but he was apparently intended to benefit (mainly psychologically) from its more visually pleasing and healing qualities. Those may be found only in areas distant from civilization. Rodman also resembles many of Poe's other protagonists in his initial gloomy outlook, though Poe may have intended to transform him into a far more balanced, positive character. Thus Rodman takes rank with the narrators in "A Descent into the Maelström" and "The Pit and the Pendulum," or young Pennifeather in "Thou Art the Man," or the questing knight in "Eldorado," in that he may have evaded the actual death or death-in-life that befell so many other Poe protagonists. The surprise element throughout *Rodman*, understandable in explorations of new regions, lacks the dynamic we find in that same technique in the earlier novel. The characters in *Rodman* also lack much depth, possibly because Poe depended so heavily on his sources instead of more strongly using his own creative imagination. He may also have used the journal method in structuring *Rodman* because he had no firm plan when he commenced writing the work. He could improvise, if necessary, but any inclination he may have had for extending the work diminished before he had written enough to give readers a sense of what might follow in future installments.

*Eureka: A Prose Poem* (1848) grew out of Poe's lectures on the nature of the universe. In the lectures and the book he drew heavily on nebular theories, another interesting branch of science in his day. Although *Eureka* has been viewed as containing the key to "all Poe," as it were, and although its scientific trappings might impute to Poe an amazing command of science, there are far too many comic insinuations throughout the book for us to deem it a major contribution to scientific thought. Thus it resembles *Pym* or tales such as "The System of Dr. Tarr and Professor Fether" (1845) or "Hans Pfaall" (1835), "The Balloon Hoax" (1844), or the mesmeric tales, "A Tale of the Ragged Mountains" (1844), "Mesmeric Revelation" (1844) and "The Facts in the Case of M. Valdemar" (1845), "The Sphinx" (1846), or the alchemical tale "Von Kempelen and His Discovery" (1849). For all Poe provides just enough scientific (or pseudo-scientific) material to play to then-current fads, he undercuts scientific accuracy with satiric touches.

Similarly, despite its echoings of Poe's critical principles, notably those championing unity and plot, *Eureka* may not be the culmination of his other critical thoughts, as has been sometimes hypothesized. One must not forget that, no matter to what artistic high peaks Poe attained, he spent most of his professional career editing and publishing in periodicals. Another signal point to remember: if any one demon may be said to have relentlessly tormented Poe, that demon was poverty. Concerns over financial stability comprised Poe's worries from the early 1830s on to his death in late 1849. Consequently, he consciously sought to publish what would pay, and, most notably in regard to his fiction, his attempts demonstrate variety. To a cursory view such variety may seem more recognizable than that among Poe's poems, which have far too often been dismissed as of a piece, which displays only sound without, or with very little, intellectual substance. Poe's writings may involve somewhat limited materials, but if his materials are limited the way he employs them may remind us of Jane Austen's remark that she very attentively polished her small bit of ivory – the materials for her novels.

To illustrate, how many general readers – or among those who have not read, but may believe, regardless, that they know something about Poe (who are perhaps familiar with "The Raven" or "The Cask of Amontillado") – are aware that Poe also published "Silence – A Fable," "Shadow – a Parable," "Ulalume" or "Eldorado"? Or that he published many book reviews, or that he published novels and *Eureka*? Such unawareness is as widespread as Poe's own reputation (and the pretenses of knowing the facts about the man and his writings), even though many texts, selective and collective, make these works available. My point is, however, that Poe wrote what he calculated would remunerate him, thereby leaving us a legacy of works that are far more heterogeneous than they are homogeneous – unless, of course, we know that so many of his creative writings might loosely be grouped under headings such as "horror," "terror" or "Gothic." That he managed to produce so many creative works, brief though they may be, while he spent so much time and energy in thankless editorial drudgery and reviewing books that often were simply dreadful, for which he was anything but overpaid, is the real miracle in his career.

## The criticism

Poe's critical writings are numerous, but, unlike many critical-theoretical works today, his did not appear in book form. They were scattered through pages of American magazines and newspapers from the 1830s to the 1850s. Most of Poe's criticism appeared in book reviews, though he did publish several topical essays, mainly concerning poetry and poetics. Despite the voluminous quantity of his criticism, Poe tended to repeat his aesthetic principles, mostly those pertaining to poetry or to the short story, so his criticism requires no prolonged explication in a book of this scope. He is best remembered for his theories of poetry and of the short story, though later writers have employed techniques different from those he championed. Several of Poe's reviews and essays have become stock anthology pieces, for example "The Philosophy of Composition" and his reviews of Hawthorne's stories, selected mainly to illustrate his definitions of poetry and the short story, but the majority of Poe's critical writings remain less familiar.

Before turning to his critical ideas proper, we should take account of the historical framework for Poe the literary critic. He was different from many other American reviewers in his day because his critical writings, like his short stories, were modeled on those that had been appearing in such British literary periodicals as the *Edinburgh Review*, the *Quarterly Review*, *Blackwood's Edinburgh Magazine* or *Fraser's Magazine*. Reviews in those publications were frequently far more virulent than critiques by American reviewers tended to be. The tameness, by way of contrast, in many American book reviews resulted from the intense literary nationalism prevalent in the early nineteenth century.

Such nationalist sentiment sympathized with American writers' lacking the centuries-long traditions of culture underlying European writing, so almost any book by an American was likely to receive a positive verdict. Publishing conditions at that time were such that prices of European books were much less than those produced in America. This financial condition in turn discouraged many Americans from becoming creative writers, and so those who did venture into the literary marketplace were, for the most part, naturally given sympathetic treatment by reviewers.

Poe was no subscriber to notions that just because something was written by an American and published in America it was bound to be wonderful. Instead, having a far more cosmopolitan outlook, and, in general, devolving from Platonic and Aristotelian principles, he assessed merits and demerits in works he reviewed. His critical viewpoints, especially those concerning poetry and the short story, tended to be far more systematic than those espoused by many of his contemporaries. Consequently, when he began to review books for the *Southern Literary Messenger*, he showed no mercy to what he thought was dreariest trash, though many of his reviews are evenly balanced in outlook.

One of Poe's most relentless onslaughts appears in his review of Theodore S. Fay's egregious novel *Norman Leslie, a Tale of the Present Times* (1835). Poe questioned Fay's methods (or lack thereof) in character creation, knowledge of proceedings in court trials, and abilities to use appropriate syntax and diction. Moreover, Poe's satiric tone in pointing out passages of what he deemed egregious expression made this review all the more insulting. Poe's mocking of Fay's tediously repeated "blistering" by repeating that word in increasingly satiric phrases within the review concluded: "if ever we saw as silly a thing, may we be – blistered" (*E&R* 548). A reader of this venomously comic review would probably not hasten to read *Norman Leslie*, so not the author's reputation alone, but the sales potential as well, would suffer.

Poe may also have published such hard-hitting reviews as that of Fay to call attention to himself as a man of letters so young but possessed of astute literary principles, and correspondingly that his capability to review, as well as the quality in his creative writings must respectively be unimpeachable and supremely artistic. Fay, and some others (e.g. Morris Mattson) whose books Poe savaged, being darlings of the powerful New York City literary establishment, brought about formulations of revenge strategies among that publishing center's writers and editors, by whom Poe was eventually repaid in kind, and more, and often when they knew that he no longer had a ready forum in which to respond.[18]

In another early review (this one not vicious but not overflowing with compliments), of William Gilmore Simms's novel *The Partisan* (1835), Poe denigrated Simms's techniques in characterization for producing too many of what we have since learned to call flat characters, though he did note several outstanding exceptions. Poe also censured the "bad taste" in several scenes, notably that in which the maniac Frampton drowns the villainous British Sergeant Hastings. In such incidents, Poe wrote, Simms tended to dwell upon the repulsive, what Poe termed "that mere *physique* of the horrible" (*E&R* 901). Surely this is an irony from one whose own works have been downgraded (unjustly) for gruesome details. Poe was subsequently to publish more commendable responses to Simms's works, and Simms in turn found much value in many of Poe's poems and tales.

Since Poe's own creative writings were chiefly brief, he tended to compliment brief works by other authors. This predilection led him to be short-sighted about the novel or the long poem. For instance, Poe persisted in a greater liking for Charles Dickens's short stories than for his novels, which are usually ranked as his greatest art. This is not to say that every novel Poe reviewed was castigated; on the contrary, his remarks about long works of fiction were often quite cogent, noting excellences as well as defects. For example, in reviewing *Sheppard Lee* (1836), a novel by the Philadelphian Robert Montgomery Bird, author of several novels and plays, Poe complimented the realistic language and Bird's ability to fashion well-wrought incidents of "force, brevity, and a species of *directness*" (*E&R* 401).

Consistent with his ideas about brevity, Poe commended the brevity he encountered in Bird's novel. He found defects, however, in the theme of metempsychosis, stating that such transmigrations as Lee, a first-person narrator, went through could have been dispensed with, with multiple narrators used to greater advantage for presenting the individual episodes. The "jocular manner" throughout did not mingle well with the dream structure for Sheppard's changes, Poe added, because it weakened verisimilitude. One wonders whether Poe found Bird's methods too like his own combinations of horror with humor in the Folio Club tales. *Sheppard Lee* is strikingly reminiscent of "Loss of Breath," where metempsychosis mingles with horror and comedy to burlesque the staple Gothic tale in *Blackwood's*. One must not be misled, however, into thinking that Poe attacked or severely qualified every book by an American that came to him to review. He simply responded antagonistically to what he interpreted as unthinking American literary nationalism because he thought it tended to foster inferior art.

Poe did not censure, or give measured praise to, these American novels only because he was wary of literary nationalism. His viewpoint also ran counter to much accepted opinion, for example when he charged the English author Edward Bulwer-Lytton with poor writing in his novel *Night and Morning*

(1841). Poe's analysis justified his strictures on that book. Much more to Poe's critical liking was Bulwer-Lytton's earlier novel, *Rienzi, the Last of the Tribunes* (1836). There Poe found superior characterization and plot technique, and excellent written expression, making this novel not only better than *Night and Morning*, but also surpassing in all respects Bulwer-Lytton's far more popular novel, *The Last Days of Pompeii* (1834), an amazing best-seller. This was great commendation for *Rienzi*, as well as testimony to Poe's alert perceptions in evaluating these books. For Poe, Bulwer-Lytton's novels in no way rose to the artistic level of Charlotte Brontë's *Jane Eyre* (1847), which he admired. Earlier he had censured E. P. Whipple, whom he considered to be a generally good critic, for his low estimate of Brontë's novel (*E&R*, respectively 1452, 1039).

Because Poe so much wanted to be recognized as a poet, his conception of poetry should be assessed here. For him, the chief end of poetry was pleasure, not truth, as he stated in the "Letter to Mr. B— —," prefatory to the 1831 *Poems*. Restatements of this idea echoed in a rewrite of that essay, as "Letter to B——," in the *Southern Literary Messenger* (1836), in another *Messenger* review of poems by two American writers, Joseph Rodman Drake and Fitz-Greene Halleck (1836), in a review of Henry Wadsworth Longfellow's *Ballads and other Poems* (1842), in "The Philosophy of Composition" (1846) and, more fully set forth, in "The Poetic Principle" (published posthumously, 1850). Although some of the thoughts expressed in these essays may also be found, wholly or in part, elsewhere among his critiques, these pieces themselves might be considered as core reading for understanding Poe's conception of poetry and the poetic (they are conveniently accessible for present-day readers in *E&R*).

In the Drake-Halleck review, after deploring American tendencies to claim excellence for American writings solely because they were American, as well as for purposes of outlining his conception of poetry, Poe resorted to borrowing what he considered would be illustrative terminology from phrenology, a pseudo-science in which the shape of the human head was deemed a gauge of one's intellectual and emotional abilities, what artistic or temperamental makeup, etc. a person possessed. Although the phrenological allusions hinder ready accessibility to Poe's aesthetic intent, we learn that poetry appeals to human instinct for appreciating the forms of beauty and to a desire to seek and comprehend ideal beauty. Assisting these pursuits is the imagination, the part of the human mind that promotes creativity. Poe derived this last idea from the theoretical writing of English Romantic poet-critic Samuel Taylor Coleridge.

For Poe, the pleasure afforded by poetry is related to music, and the necessity for musical effect in poetry is also emphasized in these essays. The musical sounds in a poem contribute to readers' or hearers' pleasure by stimulating their sense of beauty. Such beauty is ideal, not physical (this is Platonic thought), and human yearning after the beautiful is consonant with an awareness of the imperfections that are part of being human. Poe's most concise statement of this desire for beauty is found in "The Poetic Principle" (1850):

> An immortal instinct, deep within the spirit of man, is thus, plainly, a sense of the Beautiful. This it is which administers to his delight in the manifold forms, and sounds, and odours, and sentiments amid which he exists . . . [T]his is the desire of the moth for the star. It is no mere appreciation of the Beauty before us – but a wild effort to reach the Beauty above . . . Inspired by an ecstatic prescience of the glories beyond the grave, we struggle by multiform combinations among the things and thoughts of Time, to attain a portion of that Loveliness whose very elements, perhaps, appertain to eternity alone . . . [Partly] through a certain, petulant, impatient sorrow at our inability to grasp *now,* wholly, here on earth, at once and forever, those divine and rapturous joys, of which *through* the poem, or *through* the music, we attain to but brief and indeterminate glimpses.    (*E&R* 76–77)

Consequently poetry stimulates the emotions rather than the rational intellect: "The struggle to apprehend the supernal Loveliness . . . has given to the world all that which it (the world) has ever been enabled at once to understand and to feel as poetic" (*E&R* 77). Poe's conception of poetry, tersely defined in his April 1842 *Graham's Magazine* review of Longfellow's *Ballads* as "the *Rhythmical Creation of Beauty*" (*E&R* 688), and restated in this later essay (*E&R* 78), bears out his emphasis on the union of sound and sense. Long afterward, although he did not cite Poe, A. E. Housman, also a poet, expressed essentially the same idea of what constituted poetry. Delivering the annual Leslie Stephen Lecture in early 1933 at Cambridge University, published as *The Name and Nature of Poetry* (1933), Housman harked back to works by many earlier poets who were essentially Romantic in nature. Like Poe's, Housman's conception was that the foundations of poetry originated in emotions, and that a poem should convey that emotionalism. Housman's lecture was delivered partly as a twitting of writers who desired a more rational intellectual basis for poetry, though not one that would have dwindled into the didacticism that Poe so resented. Poe would doubtless have been amused by Housman's stringent humor directed toward many who were new poets in the early twentieth century, and whose conceptions of poetry differed markedly from his own – and from Poe's.

Poe thought that too much American verse was not genuine poetry at all because it tended to instruct more than to inspire the emotions. To be sure, the notion that poetry should instruct was part of the English poet Wordsworth's poetic creed, but Poe dismissed that kind of thinking. He castigated much American verse as displaying the "heresy of the didactic," that is, being too preachy-teachy at the expense of emotion. To Poe, much of Henry Wadsworth Longfellow's corpus was particularly censurable on these grounds, as was James Russell Lowell's "A Legend of Brittany," a popular poem in 1844 (*E&R* 812). He also found other American versifiers, as he implicitly classified such writers, equally liable to censure for turning out such writings.

Poe was far less strident about didacticism, however, when he reviewed poems by William Cullen Bryant (*E&R* 441) or when he cited those of John Greenleaf Whittier. Even less consistent with his high standards was his repeated acclaim for the verse of Amelia Welby, which surely fell far below his standards for genuine poetry. Welby's poems were popular during the 1840s, though they reveal no such unity of impression or effect, nor the rhythmic achievements, as Poe attributed to them. Because of his own ideas about what poetry should be – and what it should not – and his antagonistic comments about much American verse, it is not surprising that Poe's poetic theories were not met with unmitigated good will. During the mid-1840s, when Longfellow's work had immense sales, Poe's animosity, inflamed, no doubt, by acute awareness of his precarious finances and Virginia's tuberculosis, broke forth in a series of articles that offered challenges, all of which has been called the "Longfellow War."[19]

At this same time Poe incurred additional wrath because he appeared, intoxicated, before an audience in the Boston Lyceum, where he had been invited to lecture on poetry. Instead, whether from nervousness or deliberate arrogance, he delivered a few relevant observations, then spent far more time reading "Al Aaraaf," which he substituted for the requested original poem. His demeanor and the obscure, difficult subject matter in the poem (not one for extended reading to an already tired audience, as his was after hearing a lengthy speech by a previous speaker) bewildered and angered many listeners, who took umbrage at what they thought was his intentional buffoonery and mockery. Another journalistic "war" ensued, providing one more milestone in lowering Poe's reputation and credibility in yet another important publishing center. He did nothing to alleviate such hostility by responding that he had planned his performance as a hoax on his audience.

Moving on from some accounts of literary history relevant to Poe as critic, I repeat that Poe the writer desired, first and foremost, to be a poet because the poet was esteemed as the greatest kind of creative writer. Poe himself wrote that for him poetry was a "passion," stating that idea indirectly in his "Letter to Mr. B— —," which prefaced his *Poems* (1831), again in the poem "Israfel," where the speaker scoffs at "unimpassioned song," claiming that the angel-poet, Israfel, would despise such inferior verse, and that that viewpoint is the "wisest" (*M* 1: 176), and, finally, in the "Preface" to *The Raven and Other Poems* (1845), emphasizing there that with him poetry was "not a purpose, but a passion; and the passions should be held in reverence." The context in this statement meant ideal, not sensual passion. Passion may mean "ardent affection," according to Webster, and though ardent it need not involve the physical. Poe concluded that for him poetry was above mere payment in money or the opinions of critics. This last statement might be ironic, because Poe was certainly not shy about pointing out what he considered flaws in the stylistics of many other poets' productions. Nor was he reluctant to call attention to his own writings and projects, in hopes of gaining sales or other support.

Poe's repeated claims for music's being essential to poetry merits some attention because it bears on another of his aesthetic principles. The musical elements in poetry would have contributed to his insistence that a long poem was a contradiction in terms. Such contradiction resulted because no pitch, in choral or instrumental performance, could be prolonged without losing intensity (electrically powered musical instruments were not yet invented). To be dynamic, a poem had to be short, Poe contended, because music is inherently brief. Brevity correlated, too, with another of his aesthetic principles, that what really distinguished creative literary art from other writing were undercurrents of meaning or implication; those suggestions strongly contributed a depth in texture that was not found in, and that should not be part of, non-literary writing. That suggestiveness and symbolism went hand in hand, and thus true literary art admits of multiple but equally valid interpretations. Readers and listeners, being human, could only briefly sustain such suggestions or impressions as those residing in genuine literary art. Thus the excitement a poem inspired was coupled with indefiniteness. The result: emotional stimulation, not intellectual information. Poe found that indefiniteness in many of Tennyson's poems, and for that reason he ranked him the greatest of all poets (*E&R* 1331). On like grounds Poe lashed out at James Russell Lowell's "A Fable for Critics" (1848) for its "rambling plot (if plot it can be called) and for the want of artistic finish." The versification was also faulty, he thought (*E&R* 816–17, 820). Poe's ire may have been aroused by the satiric lines about him – "Three fifths of him genius, and two fifths sheer fudge," "Who has written some things far the best of their kind;/ But somehow the heart seems squeezed out by the mind." Poe also pointed out that he was the only Southern writer mentioned in the "Fable," as if to question Lowell's knowledge and objectivity about American writers and writing.

Another reason that Poe regarded brevity as the keystone element in poetry (and fiction and drama, though he did not publish as much about plays as he did about other kinds of literature) originated in his keen awareness of human psychology, with special sensitivity to the average human attention span. To Poe, that span could not extend more than an hour and a half (if that). In reviewing Nathaniel Hawthorne's short stories, in 1847, Poe contended that a poem "must intensely excite [but that] excitement is, from a psychal necessity, transient" (*E&R* 584–85). Engagement with long works could not be confined to a single sitting, so diversions necessarily intervened, a reader's attention was perforce diverted, and unity of effect was lost.

Poe's advocacy of the short story as superior to longer fiction continues to draw attention to another important segment of his critical outlook. His conception of the short story actually differs little from that for a poem: in fiction brevity is essential because it contributes to unity. This opinion first appeared in his review of Dickens's *Watkins Tottle, and other Sketches, illustrative of every-day Life, and every-day People* (1836), where Poe expressed disbelief that "less actual ability is required in the composition of a really good 'brief article,' than in a fashionable novel of the usual dimensions," adding that "unity of effect . . . is indispensable in the 'brief article,' and not so in the common novel" (*E&R* 205). Poe would continue to declare that unity of effect was crucial to genuine plot in fiction, which, following Aristotelian doctrine, he defined, in reviewing Bulwer-Lytton's *Night and Morning* (1841), as "*that in which no part can be displaced without ruin to the whole*" (*E&R* 148, Poe's italics). Such "infinite perfection which the true artist bears ever in mind" is, of course, impossible to achieve. In both poetry and tales he attempted to achieve unity of effect, i.e. well-wrought plot: in addition a lyric impulse enlivens many passages in his fiction, and his characterizations are also psychologically plausible. The majority of Poe's poems, stories and *Pym* are infused with a dramatic spirit, which may have comic or tragic thrusts, witness, as several among many examples, "The Raven," "The Fall of the House of Usher," "The Angel of the Odd" and "The Premature Burial."

That Poe deliberately turned to writing short fiction because his volumes of poems were no great successes, and that most of his short stories were cast in the terror-tale mode as bids for sales, has long been recognized. Nevertheless he rapidly divined how to write better terror (now called Gothic) fiction than most of his contemporaries. An outstanding exception was Nathaniel Hawthorne, whose volumes of short stories Poe reviewed with approval. Poe was unaware of Hawthorne's first novel, *Fanshawe* (1828), because Hawthorne had so firmly suppressed his authorship of that book that long after his death many who knew him well knew nothing of the novel's existence. *The Scarlet Letter* (1850) appeared in the year after Poe's death, and so Poe knew only Hawthorne's short fiction.

Poe's reviews of *Twice-Told Tales* appeared in the April and May 1842 issues of *Graham's Magazine*, that of *Twice-Told Tales* and a later collection of stories, *Mosses from an Old Manse*, in *Godey's Lady's Book* for November 1847. Collectively, these three critiques epitomize Poe's theory of the short story or, as he preferred, tale. In the first, and brief, notice Poe opened with the claim that the tale artistically surpasses the novel because tales "afford the best prose opportunity for display of the highest talent," adding that it "is, of course, a far finer field than the essay. It has even points of superiority over the poem" (*E&R* 568). This last statement is a surprising admission, since in reviewing Longfellow's *Ballads and other Poems*, in the April 1842 *Graham's*, Poe would champion poetry. In another remark in the April 1842 *Graham's* – that few American short stories are "of high merit," Washington Irving's in *Tales of a Traveller* (1824) excepted – Poe's accuracy is teamed with his refusal to endorse what he thought was a parochial American literary nationalism. Another statement, that some pieces are not, strictly, tales but essays, though that fact does not take away from their art, evinces a latitudinarian outlook that motivated Poe's own practices. For example, "The Murders in the Rue Morgue" commences as if it might be an essay on psychology, as do those with scientific trappings of other sorts, e.g. "Hans Pfaall," *Pym*, "Mesmeric Revelation," "The Facts in the Case of M. Valdemar," "The Sphinx" and "Von Kempelen and His Discovery." Hawthorne's accomplishments in "incident" (what we call psychological plausibility today) are noteworthy.

In the May *Graham's* review Poe repeated and expanded what he had written the previous month, once again commending Hawthorne's achievements in tone, unity of effect, novelty and original thought. In his sketches he rises superior to Lamb, Hunt and Hazlitt, as well as to the essays in the *Spectator*. Clearly, too, "unity of effect or impression is of the greatest importance" in the prose tale, which must be brief to be tightly structured. The hour-and-a-half limit in reading time is again mentioned as the ideal span for comprehending such "*totality*" (*E&R* 570ff, Poe's italics). Poe then reiterates his belief that Beauty is the province of the poem, whereas Truth is that of the tale. Writers who attempt the beautiful in their prose tales may be setting up a severe limitation; "terror, or passion, or horror" fare much better in prose-fiction renderings. Poe's allusion to the error some readers make in disparaging the fine tales of effect in early issues of *Blackwood's* reveals his own accurate understanding of such fiction, while it simultaneously, if implicitly, turns the spotlight on his own customary wares. Like the *Blackwood's* Gothic tale, many of his own were built upon "impressions [that] were wrought in a legitimate sphere of action, and constituted a legitimate although sometimes exaggerated interest" (*E&R*

573). Among Americans, Irving and Hawthorne, and to a lesser degree John Neal, have written the finest tales.

In his last review of Hawthorne, in *Godey's* for November 1847, Poe repeats most of his previous observations about the short tale's offering "the fairest field which can be afforded by the wide domains of mere prose, for the exercise of the highest genius" (*E&R* 584). Again he praises Irving and Hawthorne as American masters in tale writing, adding William Gilmore Simms's "Grayling; or, Murder Will Out" (1842) as one of America's finest short stories. Unity of effect and the brevity necessary to achieve that quality are once more outlined. Hawthorne's style is excellent because it is natural, for the most part. Poe does object to Hawthorne's tendencies to allegory in his tales, then seems to bring that objection to an abrupt end (*E&R* 583). Because of convincing arguments that Poe's own "The Masque of the Red Death" grew out of his knowing Hawthorne's 1842 *Twice-Told Tales*, most firmly from those tales grouped as "Legends of the Province-House," we may ask if Poe's bringing up the topic of allegory in this late review may allude to that cross-fertilization, so to speak.[19] Whether he mentioned allegory to suggest that Hawthorne's tales might be inferior to his own "Masque" (which some have termed allegorical), but also to call attention to the connection for other purposes, we cannot determine, but there seems to be a coded significance in the paragraphs focusing on allegory in this review.

Poe's criticism may be said to serve two major purposes, whatever additional importance may attach to that body of his writing. First, he did express critical-analytical thoughts that arose from his appreciation of and perceptions about general literary matters that interested him and about works that came to him for review. This part of his criticism is treated in preceding paragraphs. Second, no matter how accurate about artistic qualities in literature he may have been, some of Poe's best-remembered critical pieces may carry self-referential implications. In what follows I will address those features in his criticism. His dicta on poetry and the short story may give a sense of systematic thinking about each form, but such thinking puts forth as seminal artistry the very kinds of poems and tales that constitute his own highest accomplishments.

When, for instance, Poe writes in various critical works that the death of a beautiful woman is the most poetic of all themes, he may be wryly calling attention to himself by means of a specialty type within his corpus. Such methodology becomes clearer if we read that the death of a beautiful woman is the most *Poe*-etic of all themes (my emphasis). He often engaged wordplay on his own name, and since several of his literary creations did revolve around the death of a beautiful woman he may have tried enterprisingly to boost his own importance as an author and his sales in the book trade. Possibly the outstanding example of this self-promotion resides in that oft-reprinted essay "The Philosophy of Composition" (1846). This essay is a follow-up to the popularity Poe gained from "The Raven," setting forth what at face value seems to be a disclosure of why he chose the theme he chose, and how he wrote the poem, with specifics concerning the purpose of the sound effects: all was presented as if he had calmly and objectively prepared a mental outline of the poem, then set to work, very carefully and methodically, to write down the piece. The existence of several manuscript drafts of "The Raven" may plausibly lead one to question how serious Poe was in composing his explanatory essay, just as it undercuts Poe's statements elsewhere in his critical writings where poetry is defined and its purpose outlined. There may be more impishness in "The Philosophy of Composition" than many instructors and anthologists have allowed when they use it to illustrate techniques in creative writing.

If in fact "The Raven" is a poem that was written not to excite, but to exist in planes of melancholy (which by definition more nearly resembles depression than excitement), then Poe's fairly lofty tone in the essay must not be taken at face value. This thought is not intended to take away from the art in Poe's poem, a convincing rendering of how an individual's emotional disintegration leads to some fantastic speculations. Those speculations in turn end in the tragedy of death-in-life. The collapse of his mind affects his body too, bringing about immobility and silence as the poem concludes, as I have already remarked in my analysis of "The Raven" earlier in this chapter. The hypnotic sounds work upon him so firmly that he is literally left entranced by the close of the poem.

Although "The Philosophy of Composition" may resonate with as much comic as serious purpose, Poe's comments elsewhere in his critical writings may not have been expressed as they were without some measure of self-serving intent. The "Letter to Mr. B——" in *Poems* (1831) may have come into existence hopefully to bring major attention to Poe's own most characteristic type of poem. The same might be said about his many declarations that the short story was the greatest form of fiction, or even, excepting the poem, the greatest of all literary forms. These pronouncements typically followed upon Poe's own experiments with whichever genre or part of a genre he was touting. As he wrote early in his career, to Thomas White (*O* 58), "To be appreciated, you must be *read*, and these things are invariably sought after with avidity." Although by "things" Poe meant Gothic tales, his awareness of the marketplace value of being read might well apply to his thinking about much else that he wrote. The notices of individual selections within issues of the *Southern Literary Messenger*, reprinted in excerpts in issues of that magazine, repeatedly attest Poe's eagerness for publicity, albeit they are reprinted in the interests of boosting the magazine's circulation.

Poe's "Preface" to *Tales of the Grotesque and Arabesque* (1840), where he responded to those who had chided him for publishing "German," or too extravagant or horrific tales, was no mere petulance toward negative opinion. Poe's maintaining that he found terror in the soul rather than in any sleazy Germanism is an astute defense of the firm psychological foundation upon which he constructed his tales. True, his theory might also have much farther reaching application. His advertisements for his projected literary magazines were also calculated to place him in the limelight, and his displeasure over the in-house editor's choices of the twelve tales that went into *Tales* (1845), for Wiley and Putnam's "Library of American Books" series resulted from his own opinions that he knew best what was outstanding among his works. The biographical account in the Philadelphia *Saturday Museum*, in early 1843, grew out of notes that Poe supplied to Henry B. Hirst for the preparation of that article, a mix of fact and fiction. The (self-)aggrandizing of Edgar A. Poe is clear-cut to those who are in the know, though the inclusion of encomiums from prestigious authors may suggest that here are objective tributes to a truly superb writer. Poe's letters often include passages of self-promotion, which sometimes also reveal his salesman's tactics, letters where he writes that a piece just finished or just about to appear exceeds the quality of material already in print. I realize that what I outline may not place Poe as a wholly disinterested critic. But then conditions in his life, which were often desperate, were what prompted his resorting to such ploys to secure fame and fortune.

*Chapter 4*

# Reception

From his time to ours, reception of Poe has been mixed. The persistent attempts to see his personal life and his writings as inextricably linked have been the informing spirit in many biographical accounts and in certain critical approaches, whether the topic encompasses just one work or a plurality. Poe himself initiated some of the misleading biographical accounts, first in the information he provided for Griswold's *The Poets and Poetry of America* (1842, often reprinted), a long-respected anthology of American verse. Even longer, the sketch in the Philadelphia *Saturday Museum* (1843) was based on materials supplied by Poe to Henry B. Hirst. Although that piece contains significantly revised texts for some of Poe's poems, it is not wholly reliable in sections of what might be thought factual biography. Poe also sent material that contained inaccuracies to James Russell Lowell for a biographical essay in the February 1845 *Graham's Magazine*. If these articles were favorable portrayals of Poe, Griswold's maligning portraiture in his obituary notice, signed "Ludwig," of Poe in the 9 October 1849 New York *Daily Tribune* and in the expanded memoir in his edition of Poe's *Works* (1850–56) seemed to take a stronger hold on public opinion. Griswold's deviousness went long unsuspected because he did present what he considered to be the best texts for Poe's poems and fiction, though not for some of the "Literati" papers and for Poe's letters. Who would have imagined that Griswold, the meticulous editor of literary texts and respected editor of important books, could have played fast and loose with other sections of the edition to color Poe's reputation with lurid dyes? Or that such vilifying included the lifting verbatim of a passage depicting Francis Vivian, an unsympathetic character in Edward Bulwer-Lytton's novel *The Caxtons*, which had run serially in *Blackwood's* (1846–49)? The bit of fiction lifted by Griswold went unnoticed for what it was until Arthur Hobson Quinn set the record straight in his biography of Poe (1941). What an irony that a passage from one of his favorite literary magazines should be used against Poe! Griswold's vilification of his subject's character spawned many other overviews in which Poe is unfavorably portrayed, sometimes in connection with drunkenness, drug addiction or other causes that made him seem half-demonic.

More important in terms of contemporaneous reception may be the notices, however terse some of the earliest among them are, that treat Poe's writings. Unlike what exists for many other American writers of his era, Poe's publications have nowhere near the numbers of reviews that have been tabulated for publications by Hawthorne, Melville, Henry James or Mark Twain, to cite only nineteenth-century American writers. The publishers of his early volumes of poems were not prestigious, as the Harper's firm was, and so there was no great promotional drive for these books. *Tamerlane and Other Poems*, published in Boston during June or July 1827, by Calvin F. S. Thomas, had this line in the "Preface": "The greater part of the Poems, which compose this little volume, were written in the year 1821–2, when the author had not completed his fourteenth year" (*M* 1: 21). In tandem with an additional comment that the shorter pieces originated in egotism, these revelations were no strong lure for readers. Any reviewer who may have seen the book must have felt no compulsion to evaluate the contents; the book was merely listed in the August *United States Review and Literary Gazette* and in the October *North American Review*. *Al Aaraaf, Tamerlane, and Minor Poems*, published toward the close of 1829, drew more attention, either for individual poems or as a volume, though the responses were checkered. John Neal's opinions, expressed in regard to manuscript and then published versions of the contents, was that the young writer showed promise of becoming a fine poet. Baltimore reviewers were more sympathetic; although they noted faults in certain poems, they found Poe's originality refreshing. The 1831 *Poems* attracted scant notice, and what did appear gave no high kudos to the poems, excepting "To Helen," which pleased the reviewer in the 8 July *Morning Courier and New-York Enquirer*.

If the books of poetry failed to attract great notice, the appearance of Poe's critical reviews and tales in the *Southern Literary Messenger* during 1835–36 certainly won attention. In a bid for circulation increases, no doubt, the *Messenger* reprinted many notices of its individual monthly issues, culled chiefly from newspapers. These notices provide a spectrum of opinions, which ran from praise for the critical acumen in Poe's reviews to censure for some being too caustic (notably those of Fay's *Norman Leslie* or Simms's *The Partisan*). More positive were comments about Poe's art in tales containing zesty humor ("Lionizing," "Loss of Breath" and "The Duc de L'Omelette") and fine romantic fiction ("MS. Found," "The Visionary"). Several critics deplored what they considered Poe's lamentable propensities for "German" doom and gloom ("Berenice," "Morella"). "To Helen" and "The Coliseum" were several times applauded, the scenes from *Politian* dismissed as tepid.

Despite any negative opinions, Poe's writings were a main attraction in the 1835–36 issues of the *Messenger*; consequently his name soon became that of a valued American author. Once he relocated to publishing centers in the northeast, his reputation increased. *The Narrative of Arthur Gordon Pym* was expanded and published in hardcover by the renowned New York firm of Harpers in 1838, and republished in England. Reviewers were unsure whether to read the book as realistic fiction in the manner of Daniel Defoe, or to interpret it as a hoax – just what kind of hoax was uncertain. Poe's editorial employment, first with *Burton's Gentleman's Magazine*, then with *Graham's Magazine*, which offered venues for his writings, soon made older authors such as Washington Irving recommend publication of Poe's collected tales in hardcover (*Log* 271), no doubt concurring with their author's own desire to publish the short fiction in book form. That desire led to *Tales of the Grotesque and Arabesque* appearing under the imprint of Lea and Blanchard at the end of 1839 (but dated 1840) and, in turn, to generally laudatory reviews, in which Poe's accomplishments in writing humorous or horrific tales were cited. Two dissenters were James E. Heath, who worked for the *Messenger*, and who disliked Gothic fiction, and the reviewer in the *Boston Notion*, who ranked the tales "below the average of newspaper trash" (*Log* 280).

Poe's literary stature had by this time solidified enough to persuade William H. Graham, brother to George (of *Graham's Magazine*), to launch what promised to be a series, *The Prose Romances of Edgar A. Poe*, but that venture ceased after the first number, which contained "The Murders in the Rue Morgue" and "The Man That Was Used Up," a ratiocinative tale of grisly themes and a comic tale about deceptive appearances. During this same period, publication of "The Gold-Bug" as the winner in a competition sponsored by the Philadelphia *Dollar Newspaper* assisted in heightening Poe's professional profile.

The year 1845 brought about Poe's renaissance as poet after publication of "The Raven," which, with his move to the New York weekly *Broadway Journal*, immensely boosted his reputation. His part in the so-called "Longfellow War," in which he alleged that Longfellow committed plagiarism, added to his public image. The image was, however, primarily that of a curmudgeon jealous of other writers' successes. Negative effects of that controversy were compounded by Poe's drunken debacle at the Boston Lyceum and the lawsuit with Thomas Dunn English over the "Literati" papers. Poe won the court case, but he lost much credibility as a respected writer in the northeastern literary world, which had come to dislike his pugnacious attitudes and reviews. Poe's professional woes were intensified by Virginia's death in early 1847, which deeply depressed him. Scurrilous attacks in the *John-Donkey*, a New York based periodical, to which English contributed satires on Poe's person and parodies of his writings, gave Poe's reputation no quarter. Publication of *Eureka* in 1848 brought him some renown, but again readers were unsure of the exact nature of that book: was it sound scientific thought or was it another of Poe's hoaxes? Following his own death, in October 1849, which event brought forth recollections that were not always complimentary, and with publication of the first volumes of Griswold's edition of the *Works* the next year (and despite the commendatory notices by Willis and others included there), Poe's reputation was smirched, and a cloud shadowed his memory for almost a century.

Others also sprang up to defend and protect Poe's name and accomplishments. Central among these champions was Sarah Helen Whitman, the poet from Providence, Rhode Island, whom Poe considered marrying after he had become a widower. Her *Edgar Poe and His Critics* (1860), who issued a staunch defense of Poe against calumnies that emanated from Griswold's defamation. Mrs.Whitman also compared Poe with contemporary writers, and her knowledge of their literary milieu has been a valuable contribution to Poe studies. Her book is still well worth reading as an antidote to the sensationalizing associated with Poe's reputation.

Nevertheless, Poe's writings, singly or collectively, continued to appear throughout the nineteenth century, as did additional biographical accounts. Interest in the man and his works spread across the world, as the essays in Lois Davis Vines's edited collection, *Poe Abroad* (1999), bear out. Several French writers seemed to discern special affinities between Poe's writings and their own, with notable (if imprecise) translations by Baudelaire and high regard expressed in verse by Mallarmé. In Great Britain the Rossettis, A. C. Swinburne and Ernest Dowson expressed great admiration for Poe's poetry. D. G. Rossetti's "The Blessed Damozel" derives from "The Raven." Dowson's favorite line of poetry in English was "the viol, the violet, and the vine," from "The City in the Sea." Wilkie Collins's tale "The Yellow Mask" could be a rewrite of "The Masque of the Red Death," and allusions to Poe's writings crop up in various titles in John Lane's notorious "Keynotes Series" during the 1890s. When it first appeared, Bram Stoker's *Dracula* was likened to "The Fall of the House of Usher" by one reviewer, who placed it, too, in company with *The Mysteries of Udolpho, Wuthering Heights* and "Marjorie of Quether."

An Englishman, John Henry Ingram, championed Poe from the 1870s on into the early years of the twentieth century, publishing sympathetic articles, biographies (1874–75, expanded 1880) and several editions of the writings. Ingram was extremely jealous of his role as Poe's defender, and in the course of his labors he managed to offend some of Poe's other partisans, for example Mrs. Whitman, with whom he was not always straightforward in using materials she supplied to him. Two other biographers, to whose books Ingram was hostile, William F. Gill and Eugene Didier, brought out their books in

1877, which were far from objective accounts. Another testimony to Poe's greatness was created in the form of a monument, completed in 1875, in the graveyard of Westminster Presbyterian Church, in Baltimore. Poe's remains were transferred from the plot of David Poe, Sr., elsewhere in that cemetery, and placed with those of Virginia and Mrs. Clemm in a far more prominent location, amidst public ceremony and acclaim for one of the city's honored authors.

Two other editions of Poe's writings were undertaken in the late nineteenth century, in hopes of providing complete (or as complete as was possible) editions of Poe's works, which would contain accurate biographical information. The first, published in London by Kegan Paul, Trench (1884) as *The Works of Edgar Allan Poe*, in six volumes, contains R. H. Stoddard's introduction, in which he demeans the criticism and poems, but compliments the tales. Stoddard had published other, generally unsympathetic accounts of Poe, who, as editor of the *Broadway Journal*, had rejected Stoddard's submissions. This edition, reprinted in England during the 1890s without making clear that it was reprint, attracted much notice, and served as another barometer of Poe's continued popularity. The second, more comprehensive (though not complete) edition in ten volumes was that published in Chicago by Stone and Kimball and in London by Lawrence & Bullen (1894–96). Captained by Edmund C. Stedman and George E. Woodberry, the notes and apparatus were first rate for the era. Woodberry and Stedman had individually published much other material on Poe, so they were well suited to prepare this edition, which was widely reviewed in the press on both sides of the Atlantic, heralded as a fine service to Poe's accomplishments. Woodberry had, of course, written the Poe biography for the "American Men of Letters" series (1885), which he was to revise and expand into two volumes (1909). A specialist in comparative literature, and a faculty member in Columbia University, Woodberry tried to be objective as Poe's biographer, though he did not always succeed. His books were, however, in no way comparable with Griswold's viciousness, and the 1909 version contains some worthwhile criticism.

What these and many other publications from the close of the nineteenth century demonstrate is that Poe's reputation remained alive, and was more often admired than not. Reviews of various collections or reprints of individual works that appeared during the 1890s make us aware that the entire Poe canon was familiar reading, not just those few selections found repeatedly in later academic anthologies. To be sure, what one commentator found superb another might as warmly condemn. Several sequels to *Pym* suggest that that book was not languishing among readers. Poe's tales were often placed in traditions of sensation fiction, thought by some as a product chiefly of the

1860s, although sensation-fiction themes continued to infiltrate much that was published decades later.

Two events during the first decade of the twentieth century were important for Poe's reputation. In 1902 appeared the seventeen-volume *Complete Works of Edgar Allan Poe*, edited by James A. Harrison, a professor in the University of Virginia. Textual notes were supplied by one of his former students, Robert A. Stewart, whose dissertation (1901) addressed revisions in Poe's works. The edition was, however, incomplete (Harrison was unaware of portions of the Poe canon, and included some items that were not Poe's), and Stewart's notes also introduce occasional errors. This edition has remained in use, however, and has been twice reprinted (1966; 1979, with an introduction by Floyd Stovall, Edgar Allan Poe Professor of English in the University of Virginia).

A second important event was a celebration of the centenary of Poe's birth, held in Baltimore in 1909, with the keynote memorial address delivered by Professor William P. Trent, of Columbia University, a specialist in Southern literature. Another tribute – a bronze statue of Poe prepared by an American who had long lived in Rome, Sir Moses Ezekiel – was commissioned in 1911, but was not finally received and unveiled in Wyman Park, in northern Baltimore, until 20 October 1921. The statue was moved to the University of Baltimore campus, and a celebratory conference held, in the early 1980s, an appropriate relocation because the Edgar Allan Poe Society of Baltimore, founded in 1922, had long been headquartered on that campus. The new location also gave the statue greater prominence than it had enjoyed in Wyman Park. Other Poe shrines were to appear in Richmond, Philadelphia and Fordham.

Study of Poe had commenced among academics during the early years of the century, marked by publication of what were then useful anthologies such as J. H. Whitty's edition of the poems (1911), and Killis Campbell's more scholarly edition of the poems (1917) and his volume of the tales (1927). Campbell's graduate seminars on Poe during the 1920s–30s at the University of Texas spurred many of his students, for example J. G. Varner, J. R. Rhea and Arlin Turner, to publish short studies of Poe that continue to be useful. Another stimulant to reception of Poe came about during the second and third decades of the twentieth century, when Thomas Ollive Mabbott, who earned all of his academic degrees at Columbia University, where his mentor was Professor Trent, embarked on what he projected as an edition of Poe's writings that would surpass Harrison's. Ironically, after spending almost fifty years in working, though not steadily, on that edition, Mabbott died in May 1968, just after he had finished proofreading the first volume (of an anticipated ten), the poems, which appeared as part of *Collected Works of Edgar Allan Poe*, from the Belknap Press of Harvard University Press. He had completed the major work on two volumes of tales and sketches, which were then seen through to completion by Maureen Cobb Mabbott, with able assistance from Eleanor D. Kewer, an editor at Harvard. Their work was expedited by a former Mabbott student, and much-published writer herself, Patricia Edwards Clyne. Mabbott's Poe collection is now at the University of Iowa, where it is available to scholars.

Mabbott's editorial successor, Burton R. Pollin, captained five volumes of *Collected Writings of Edgar Allan Poe*, which include *The Imaginary Voyages* (*Pym*, "Hans Pfaall" and *The Journal of Julius Rodman*) (Boston: Twayne, 1981), *The Brevities* ("Pinakidia," "Marginalia," "Literary Small Talk," "Fifty Suggestions," "A Chapter of Suggestions," with supplementary "Pinakidia" and "Marginalia"), *Broadway Journal Prose* (2 vols.), and, in collaboration with J. V. Ridgely, *Southern Literary Messenger Prose* (these last four volumes with Gordian Press) between 1981 and 1997. Two volumes, *Poetry and Tales*, edited by Patrick F. Quinn, and *Essays and Reviews*, edited by G. R. Thompson, appeared in the "Library of America" series (1984). Nevertheless, there is still no complete edition of the writings of one of America's most popular and most sophisticated authors. Poe's letters have been edited by John Ward Ostrom (1948, 1966, with supplements), but a new, larger, more fully annotated edition is being prepared by Burton R. Pollin and Jeffrey A. Savoye.

To turn to other works that have proved standard to reception of Poe, I cite biographies by the novelist Hervey Allen, whose attempts to provide more accurate information resulted first in a two-volume book (1926), and then in a revised, improved edition of that work (1934), which was superseded by Arthur H. Quinn's biography (1941, last reprinted 1998), a book that was more than twenty years in the making, as Quinn amassed and sifted pertinent materials. His facts were sound; many of his critical principles are still worth considering. Since the appearance of his book, very few new facts about Poe have been discovered. Kenneth Silverman chose a decidedly Freudian interpretation for his biography (1991), but he ignored much of the criticism that had appeared in the post-Quinn interval. Silverman's thesis, that the women in Poe's life who died young were the paramount impetus for his creative writings, is subject to challenge, so Quinn's continues as the standard biography of Poe.

Although studies of Poe had appeared as books or as articles in academic journals, no single critical book of any value for Poe studies appeared until Edward H. Davidson's *Poe: A Critical Study* (1957), which encompasses the entire canon, places Poe as representative of Romanticism in his era that emphasized darker aspects in the human self, and finds Poe's poetry and fiction far more artistic than had been the general trend in many previous studies. To Davidson, Poe's creative works were experiments with motifs of journey from the everyday world into the reality of an ideal world, a topic that likewise enters into his critical writings. Poe's great limitation is the repeated topic of the self. Poe's aspects of hoax are given sensible notice. Davidson's book has been a catalyst for many subsequent critiques of Poe.

In the wake of Davidson's book came Richard Wilbur's "The House of Poe," delivered originally as a lecture for and published by the Library of Congress (1959), and reprinted several times. Arguing that Poe's creative works foreground subtle architectural symbolism, Wilbur gives special attention to the upward and downward spiral motifs that he believes are symbolic journeys into depths in the self, and that thereby enrich symbolic texture in these writings. This influential interpretation continues to stimulate new readings of Poe's writings. For several collections of Poe's poems Wilbur also furnished introductions in which he stresses how the poetry typically focuses upon spiritual journeys away from whatever is mundane, on toward an ideal world.

Poe's sources – which were one of Mabbott's longtime interests since Poe modified details and surpassed the quality in his sources – have many descendants in academic studies, many of which are not molded around the deadly parallel alone, but open windows into Poe's art. This type of study has perhaps no greater practicioner than Burton R. Pollin, who has assiduously tracked down origins for many works by Poe. Pollin's *Discoveries in Poe* (1970) collects some of his best efforts in such pursuits. Operating in another direction, Pollin has also pursued Poe's impacts upon literature and on other arts, with studies of musical renditions based on Poe's works, of illustrations based upon Poe's writings, and, of course, how Poe's writings have inspired other writers, for example Henry James, Walter de la Mare, Ernest Hemingway, James Thurber, Thomas Mann and Stephen King.

Although Pollin believes that evidential scholarship, as he calls it, is important for expanding knowledge and appreciation of Poe's works, others in academe have employed more theoretical approaches. Edward Wagenknecht, an able synthesizer of others' thoughts, enhanced by his own, produced a valuable book, especially for beginners, in *Edgar Allan Poe: The Man behind the Legend* (1963). Part of the book addresses Poe's life, part assesses his works, all from a sane viewpoint that does not veer into any fixation upon some single great point about the man or his works. A similar work, though more brief (and written according to specifications), is Vincent Buranelli's *Edgar Allan Poe*, in the Twayne American Author series (1977), which also presents a balanced approach to Poe's life and writings.

Whereas several critics in the late nineteenth and early twentieth centuries, for example Robert Louis Stevenson and Woodberry, found Poe's humorous works to be simply dreadful, remarking that he had no genuine sense of humor, greater respect for his comic techniques began in the twentieth century to supercede those earlier outlooks. Among others, Mabbott, James Southall Wilson, Walter Fuller Taylor, James W. Gargano, James M. Cox, Richard P. Benton, G. R. Thompson, Alexander Hammond, J. Gerald Kennedy, Kent Ljungquist and Benjamin F. Fisher have argued for a strong, and artistic, comic impulse at work in Poe's fiction. Some of the best critiques of Poe's humor are assembled in Dennis W. Eddings (ed.), *The Naiad Voice: Essays on Poe's Satiric Hoaxing* (1983), a volume worth consulting on such matters. Three books that initially startled many longtime Poe enthusiasts were Michael Allen's *Poe and the British Magazine Tradition* (1969), Daniel Hoffman's *Poe-PoePoePoePoePoePoe* (1972) and G. R. Thompson's *Poe's Fiction: Romantic Irony in the Gothic Tales* (1973). All foregrounded Poe as writing/publishing with a twofold intent: (a) appealing to readers who wanted to find only sensational thrills infusing the fiction they read and (b) simultaneously writing for an elite audience, who would penetrate surface horrors to hidden, but more important suggestions beneath. Origins for this dual aim came primarily from the terror tale featured so repeatedly in *Blackwood's* and other British magazines of the early nineteenth century. Allen's book was well received, more so than the other two, which were dealt unsympathetic treatment from many reviewers. Hoffman argued for internal origins of Poe's humorous outlook, like Allen showing that Poe came rapidly to observe that most of his readers were too imperceptive to fathom an author's imagination, in Poe's case an imagination inclining toward despair over much that he observed in life around him, as well as in his own. Being superior to such imperceptiveness, he manipulated conventions in horror literature to perpetrate hoaxes, though seriousness is usually present even in the most comic tales. Hoffman's breezy style displeased some readers, who perhaps did not go on to comprehend his profundity.

Thompson's book, which critiques many though not all of Poe's Gothic tales (e.g. no explication of "The System of Dr. Tarr and Professor Fether," which should be prime in such context), suggests that Poe, aware of the too apparent extravagances and improbabilities in terror tales, in situation, characterization and language, found ammunition in currents of German Romantic irony for directing satire and parody at conventional Gothic horror stories and their authors. Poe fashioned hoaxes that might simultaneously be freighted with ample seriousness, for example in "Metzengerstein," "Loss of Breath" and "The Fall of the House of Usher." A strong platform of late twentieth-century criticism follows ideas found in these books. More than Allen or Hoffman, Thompson builds on the work of earlier critics who investigated Poe's comic impulses as worthwhile elements in his fiction.

As has been true of many other writers of his generation, Poe and his writings have been examined from viewpoints that originated with Jacques Derrida and Jacques Lacan, culminating, perhaps, in books by J. Gerald Kennedy, *Poe, Death and the Life of Writing* (1987), and Michael J. S. Williams, *A World of Words: Language and Displacement in the Fiction of Edgar Allan Poe* (1988). Kennedy and Williams employ techniques of signification and deconstruction, though Kennedy draws in biographical information more than Williams. Finally, in this context, John Irwin, in *The Mystery to a Solution: Poe, Borges, and the Analytic Detective Story* (1994), also draws upon additional recent critical theory to support his own brilliant viewpoints concerning Poe's detective fiction and its affinities with that of the renowned Argentinean writer, Borges. Irwin's additional drawing upon the ancient Classics, anthropology and color symbolism, plus the dense texture of this book, may deter rapid reading, but the book sheds great illumination on detective crime fiction – and much else.

Another recent critical approach to Poe and his canon turns to racial issues. This topic has produced sharp divergences among Poe specialists. One line of argument runs that Poe wrote the "Paulding-Drayton Review," in the *Messenger* for April 1836, of two pro-slavery books, and that since the review is favorable to ideas in those books Poe himself must have been a racist. Unfortunately for that hypothesis, it was not Poe but Beverly Tucker who wrote the review, as was demonstrated as long ago as 1941, by William Doyle Hull in his PhD dissertation, University of Virginia. Some have countered that if Poe did not write the review he was the editor of the *Messenger*. Therefore he must have shared sentiments set forth not only in the review but in the two books it concerned. One cannot prove just what Poe's attitudes were, but as far as reviews, plus much else in the *Messenger*, were concerned, what White, the owner, wanted was what was published. White would not have wanted to offend a contributor so eminent as Tucker, though he did not chastise Poe for shortening the review.

The Poe/race approach has been used as a tool to analyze *The Narrative of Arthur Gordon Pym*, "The Murders in the Rue Morgue," "The System of Dr. Tarr and Professor Fether," "The Raven" and "Hop-Frog," to name those works usually contextualized under this rubric. However, if we look again at literary, and other, history, we learn that Poe's contemporaries, who were certainly attuned to ideas regarding slavery and possible slave revolts in the southern USA, ventured nary a word about any racial issues in any of Poe's works, which certainly would have been the case had readers and reviewers sensed any such context (despite any shortcomings in this wish, they wanted to be as timely as Poe himself). In addition, although Poe was certainly attentive to what current events might be milked for profitable writing, slavery, and not just that in his own nation, was of long standing. Likewise in regard to apes in his fiction. The appearance for display in zoos of great ape species was in Poe's day fairly recent in western world culture. Just as Poe did not have to murder a woman or have himself buried alive so he could write convincingly about such occurrences, it may be doubted that every time the motif of an ape entered his mind he equated that animal exclusively with an African-American.

After give-and-take had occurred in conference sessions and in several articles that promoted the Poe/race issue, Terence Whalen, in *Edgar Allan Poe and the Masses: The Political Economy of Literature in Antebellum America* (1999), produced what continues as the most objective overview of Poe and race. Whalen posits that Poe's writings offer far stronger contexts than a pro-slavery one, noting, too, that many ambiguities in *Pym* defy specific classification. The novel and several of the tales may indeed yield far more testimony to the nature of their art if one approaches them from a gender or feminist perspective than that of race, although readings based on those other lines of thought may also seem extreme. For example, the events in *Pym* strongly suggest that a dominant masculinity may create dislocation or even disaster, as in the destruction of the (feminine) ship, *Jane Guy*, by the Tsalalians, where a male ethic seems to prevail. The merger of Pym with the female symbolizes his advancing from the carefree, irresponsible adolescence that motivated him when the novel began, making him a forerunner of other American literary characters like Tom Sawyer or Huck Finn. Pym's maturing is assisted by Dirk Peters, whose makeup spans races, just as his name may hint of phallicness (which would understandably be part of Pym's maturing experience) and salvation, i.e. like St. Peter, Peters is involved with Pym's salvation – from perpetual adolescence and immaturity. Dirk Peters may be an odd recasting of the biblical Peter, but that he is may partake of Poe's hoaxing bent, which, as has been said, is not wholly divorced from seriousness. This possibility may also reinforce the Americanness in *The Narrative of Arthur Gordon Pym*, where Poe indeed paid heed to the counsel of James Kirke Paulding, but heeded in his own manner.

In sum, reception of Poe and his writings reveals that he is an author of many parts. Numerous studies are available for those who wish to expand their knowledge of Poe and his works, although much information may be too specialized for a general reader. The most recent coverage of Poe's life and career may be found in *The Cambridge Companion to Edgar Allan Poe*, ed. Kevin J. Hayes (2002). The published annual lectures, along with several books of edited essays, from the Edgar Allan Poe Society of Baltimore have also been helpful for beginners and seasoned Poe scholars alike. I close by mentioning another two important facilitators to causes of Poe: *Poe Studies/Dark Romanticism*, which under various titles has existed since 1968, and the more recent publications of the Poe Studies Association, an organization founded in 1972, which holds regular sessions during conferences of the Modern Language Association of America and the American Literature Association. A *Newsletter* was started shortly after the PSA began; in the spring of 2000 that publication was revamped into a full-fledged journal, the *Edgar Allan Poe Review*. These journals aim at circulating high-quality work on Poe, and they have been vital in promoting interest in their subject. Add the many conferences, Poe Birthday celebrations, T-shirts, drinking glasses, action figures, numerous representations of the raven, a bar on Sullivan's Island, plus the repeated allusions to Poe or to his writings in the writings of other authors, in music, in the graphic arts and in on-line references: all attest that Poe's status shows no signs of diminishing.

# Notes

## 1 Life

1 See "The Poets and Poetry of Philadelphia," *Philadelphia Saturday Museum*, 4 March 1843: 1. Poe himself supplied the information for the article to Henry B. Hirst, a Philadelphia attorney and author. This rare document, with commentary, may be found in Benjamin F. Fisher, ed., *Masques, Mysteries and Mastodons: A Poe Miscellany*. Baltimore: The Edgar Allan Poe Society, 2006: 155–93. See also reminiscences by Mary Elizabeth Bronson, published by Carroll D. Laverty, "Poe in 1847," *American Literature* 20 (May 1948): 163–68. Bronson's impression of Poe differs greatly from more negative portrayals.

2 For parallels between Poe's West Point training and his prosody, see Daniel Hoffman's "Foreward" (xiii) and William F. Hecker's "Introduction" (xxxi–xli) in *Private Perry and Mister Poe: The West Point Poems* (1831). Baton Rouge: Louisiana State University Press, 2005.

3 Poe's letter requesting such financial remuneration, 3 June 1836, to James H. Causten, who had been instrumental in settling similar claims with the federal government, did not bring the desired reimbursement. See *The Letters of Edgar Allan Poe*, ed. John Ward Ostrom. Rev. edn. New York: Gordian Press, 1966: 91–93 (hereafter cited within the text as *O*, with page numbers).

4 *Collected Works of Edgar Allan Poe*, ed. Thomas Ollive Mabbott. Cambridge, Mass.: The Belknap Press of Harvard University Press, 1968–78. 2: 18 (hereafter cited within the text as *M*, with appropriate volume and page numbers). Although Mabbott prints the final revised version of "Metzengerstein," the opening remained unchanged from the tale's first appearance, 14 January 1832; see John Grier Varner, ed., *Edgar Allan Poe and the Philadelphia* Saturday Courier. Charlottesville: University of Virginia, 1933 (which prints facsimiles of the 1832 texts): 9.

5 John Hill Hewitt, *Shadows on the Wall; or, Glimpses of the Past, a Retrospect of the Past Fifty Years*. Baltimore: Turnbull Bros., 1877: 154–57.

6 Vincent Buranelli, *Edgar Allan Poe*. 2nd edn. Boston: Twayne, 1977: 65.

7 Poe's favorable opinion of Thomas appears in "Autography," *Graham's Magazine* 19 (December 1841): 273; reprinted conveniently in *The Complete Works of Edgar Allan Poe*, ed. James A. Harrison. New York: Thomas Y. Crowell, 1902; reprinted New York: AMS Press, 1965. 15: 209–10 (hereafter cited within the text as *H*, with appropriate volume and page numbers). The quoted phrase is Arthur Hobson Quinn's, in

*Edgar Allan Poe: A Critical Biography.* New York: Appleton-Century-Crofts, 1941; reprinted with an introduction by Shawn Rosenheim. Baltimore: Johns Hopkins University Press, 1998: 323.

8 Poe to Frederick W. Thomas, 4 May 1845, in *O* 287.

## 2 Contexts

1 "Preface" to *Tamerlane and Other Poems*. By a Bostonian. Boston: Calvin S. Thomas, 1827: iii.

2 Two of the most interesting investigations are those by J. O. Bailey, "What Happens in 'The Fall of the House of Usher'?" *American Literature* 35 (1964): 445–66, and Lyle H. Kendall, Jr., "The Vampire Motif in 'The Fall of the House of Usher'," *College English* 24 (1963): 450–53. Working independently they located copies of the *Vigiliae Mortuorum Secundum Chorum Ecclesiae Maguntinae* (1500), a text used to ward off vampires, and one that many previous scholars supposed was a title devised by Poe for hoax purposes.

3 Poe's knowledge of the everyday world is attested by Ernest Marchand, "Poe as Social Critic," *American Literature* 6 (1934): 28–43; Edward Wagenknecht, *Edgar Allan Poe: The Man behind the Legend*. New York: Oxford University Press, 1963, especially chs. 2 and 3, respectively "Living" and "Learning"; and, most recently, Terence Whalen, *Edgar Allan Poe and the Masses: The Political Economy of Literature in Antebellum America*. Princeton: Princeton University Press, 1999.

4 Poe's relationships with the Southwest Humorists are critiqued by Constance Rourke, *American Humor: A Study of the National Character*. New York: Harcourt, Brace, 1931: 145–49; Harry M. Bayne, "Poe's 'Never Bet the Devil Your Head' and Southwest Humor," *American Renaissance Literary Report: An Annual* 3 (1989): 278–79; and my "Devils and Devilishness in Comic Yarns of the Old Southwest," *ESQ: A Journal of the American Renaissance* 36 (1990): 39–60.

5 See Marchand, "Poe as Social Critic," 31–33; Poe's letter to Paulding, 19 July 1838, in John Ostrom, "Fourth Supplement of the Letters of Poe," *American Literature* 45 (1974): 517–18; and Poe's letter, 3 June 1836, to James H. Causten, in regard to a pension for Elizabeth Poe (*O* 91–93).

6 Paul Woolf, "Prostitutes, Paris and Poe: The Sexual Economy of Edgar Allan Poe's 'The Murders in the Rue Morgue'," *Clues: A Journal of Detection* 25 (2006): 6–19.

7 The word appears in Poe's "Literati" sketch of Margaret Fuller, in *Godey's* for August 1846 and is conveniently located in *E&R* 1173. The coinage is cited by Burton R. Pollin, *Poe, Creator of Words*. Revised and augmented edition. Bronxville, NY: Nicholas T. Smith, 1980: 27.

## 3 Works

1 Poe's meticulousness in editorial-stylistic matters is attested in his letter, 3 October 1842, to Robert Hamilton, editor of *Snowden's Ladies' Companion*, in Joseph J.

Moldenhauer, *A Descriptive Catalog of Edgar Allan Poe Manuscripts in the Humanities Research Center Library, The University of Texas at Austin*. Austin, Texas: The University of Texas at Austin, 1973: 55–56. Worthwhile critiques plus a bibliography, by Robert W. Burns, which cites additional studies of Poe's revisions, appear in Benjamin F. Fisher, (ed.), *Poe at Work: Seven Textual Studies*. Baltimore: The Edgar Allan Poe Society, 1978.

2  See *M* 1: 22–25, 61–64 for information on the historical Tamerlane and for possible autobiographical implications in the poem.

3  Richard Wilbur's note to "Al Aaraaf," in *Poe*. Laurel Poetry Series. New York: Dell, 1959: 124–27, offers a sensible explication. See also the chapter on "Al Aaraaf" in Floyd Stovall, *Edgar Poe the Poet: Essays New and Old on the Man and His Work*. Charlottesville: University of Virginia, 1969: 102–25.

4  This concept of music appears in "Letter to Mr. B——," prefatory to *Poems* (New York: Elam Bliss, 1831); reprinted in *Edgar Allan Poe: Essays and Reviews*, ed. G. R. Thompson. New York: Library of America, 1984: 11. The statement about rhythm and beauty, from a review of Henry W. Longfellow's *Ballads and Other Poems*, originally in *Graham's Magazine* (April 1842), is reprinted in *E&R* 688. Poe reiterated many of his ideas about poetry in "The Poetic Principle," *Sartain's Union Magazine* (October 1850), reprinted in *E&R* 78. See Mabbott's headnote to the poem, *M* 1: 133–34.

5  Mabbott comments in the playfulness in these poems, citing Poe's own ideas about comic verse, expressed in "A Few Words about Brainard" (*E&R* 404–11), along with his own perceptions about humor in these poems, respectively *M* 1: 138–39, and the note to lines 41ff, which cites Shakespeare's *A Midsummer Night's Dream* as a source for "Fairy-Land" (natural that one comedy should inspire another) and 133–34 on "To the River."

6  Bettany Hughes, *Helen of Troy: Goddess, Princess, Whore*. New York: Alfred A. Knopf, 2005, especially 1–13, 342–43. Richard Wilbur also reminds us how Poe tends to emphasize the ideality of his female characters by presenting them as art figures: *Poe*, 133–35.

7  An acute biographical interpretation is Paull F. Baum's "Poe's 'To Helen'," *Modern Language Notes* 64 (1949): 289–97. Classical sources are assessed in *M* 1: 163–71. J. M. Pemberton assesses the brilliant light motif in "Poe's 'To Helen': Functional Wordplay and a Possible Source," *Poe Studies* 3.1 (December 1970): 6–7, though Pemberton's findings differ somewhat from my own.

8  Since the project has elicited controversies, several studies of the Folio Club are worth consulting. Thomas O. Mabbott, "On Poe's 'Tales of the Folio Club'," *Sewanee Review* 26 (1928): 171–76; James Southall Wilson, "The Devil Was in It," *American Mercury* 24 (1931): 215–20; Alexander Hammond, "A Reconstruction of Poe's 1833 *Tales of the Folio Club*," *Poe Studies* 5.2 (December 1972): 25–32; and his "Edgar Allan Poe's *Tales of the Folio Club*: The Evolution of a Lost Book," in Fisher, ed., *Poe at Work*: 13–43; and my *The Very Spirit of Cordiality: The Literary Uses of Alcohol and Alcoholism in the Tales of Edgar Allan Poe*. Baltimore: The Edgar Allan

Poe Society, 1978. An excellent recent examination of the heterogeneous modes of writings in *Blackwood's*, a major source for Poe's themes and techniques in fiction, is Philip Flynn, "Beginning Blackwood's: The Right Mix of *Dulce* and *Utile*," *Victorian Periodicals Review* 30.2 (Summer 2006): 136–57.

9 Texts for the sketches, along with information about Brannan, appear in Hennig Cohen and William B. Dillingham, eds., *Humor of the Old Southwest*. Athens, GA and London: University of Georgia Press, 1994: 442–47.

10 Dana Brand, "'Reconstructing the Flaneur': Poe's Invention of the Detective Story," *Genre* 18 (Spring 1985): 35–56. See also Brand's ch. 5, on Poe, in his *The Spectator and the City in Nineteenth Century American Literature*. Cambridge: Cambridge University Press, 1991.

11 A similar outreach to readers concerned with temperance appears in another tale, "The Angel of the Odd" (1844), where the narrator's drunkenness is depicted in terms of hilarity. See *M* 2: 1098–1100; and Claude Richard, "Arrant Bubbles: Poe's 'Angel of the Odd'," *Poe Newsletter* 2 (1969): 46–48; reprinted in Dennis W. Eddings, ed., *The Naiad Voice: Essays on Poe's Satiric Hoaxing*. Port Washington: Associate Faculty Press, 1983: 66–72.

12 Two of the most sensible recent approaches to this tale are Ronald Gottesman, "'Hop-Frog' and the American Nightmare"; and Ruth L. Clements, "On a Merry-Go-Round Named Denial: Critics, 'Hop-Frog,' and Poe," in Benjamin F. Fisher, ed., *Masques, Mysteries and Mastodons: A Poe Miscellany*. Baltimore: The Edgar Allan Poe Society, 2006, respectively 133–44, 145–54.

13 Paulding to Thomas W. White, 3 March 1836, and to Poe, 17 March 1836, in *The Letters of James Kirke Paulding*, ed. Ralph M. Aderman. Madison: University of Wisconsin Press, 1962, respectively 173–75, 177–78.

14 See Alexander Hammond's hypothesis on the partial emergence of *Pym* from the Folio Club Scheme, "The Composition of *The Narrative of Arthur Gordon Pym*: Notes toward a Re-examination," *American Transcendental Quarterly* 37 (Winter 1978): 9–20.

15 See *Naming Your Baby*. Columbus, Ohio: Ross Laboratories, 1991: 21.

16 Richard Kopley epitomizes theories about the white figure's implications; see n. 9 to ch. 24 in his edition of *Pym*. New York: Penguin Putnam, 1999: 242–44.

17 A refreshing, recent critique by Marita Nadal opens with her view that "Too many interpretations of *The Narrative of Arthur Gordon Pym* (1838) have already been given; in fact, it might be said that the approaches to this text are practically exhausted." "Beyond the Gothic Sublime: Poe's *Pym* or the Journey of Equivocal (E)motions," *Mississippi Quarterly* 53 (2000): 373–87. A sensible overview of the multiple perspectives on *Pym* is Ronald C. Harvey, *The Critical History of Edgar Allan Poe's* The Narrative of Arthur Gordon Pym: *"A Dialogue of Unreason."* New York and London: Garland, 1998.

18 See Sidney P. Moss, *Poe's Literary Battles: The Critic in the Context of His Literary Milieu*. Durham, NC: Duke University Press, 1963; and his *Poe's Major Crisis: His Libel Suit and New York's Literary World*. Durham, NC: Duke University Press, 1970.

My "Poe and the John-Donkey – A Nasty Piece of Work," *Essays in Arts and Sciences*, 29 (2000): 17–41, furnishes more information about particularly vicious hits at Poe by Thomas Dunn English in the *John-Donkey*, a comic weekly published for several months during 1848.

19 The Hawthorne background for Poe's tale is carefully considered in Robert Regan's "Hawthorne's 'Plagiary'; Poe's Duplicity," *Nineteenth-Century Fiction* 25 (1970): 281–98. A worthwhile brief follow-up to Regan's critique is Jerry A. Herndon's "'The Masque of the Red Death': A Note on Hawthorne's Influence," in Fisher, ed., *Masques, Mysteries and Mastodons*, 38–44.

# A guide to further reading

Allen, Michael. *Poe and the British Magazine Tradition*. New York: Oxford University Press, 1969. Important for Poe's derivations in theme and style.

Benton, Richard P. "Some Remarks on Poe and His Critics," *University of Mississippi Studies in English*, n.s. 3 (1982): i–xii. Useful overview of works about Poe from his own era to the twentieth century.

Budd, Louis J. and Edwin H. Cady. Eds. *On Poe: The Best from* American Literature. Durham, NC and London: Duke University Press, 1993. Convenient marshaling of significant critiques of Poe in this influential scholarly periodical.

Eddings, Dennis W. Ed. *The Naiad Voice: Essays on Poe's Satiric Hoaxing*. Port Washington, NY: Associated Faculty Press, 1983. Selection of important assessments of Poe's comic propensities.

Fisher, Benjamin F. Ed. *Poe at Work: Seven Textual Studies*. Baltimore: The Edgar Allan Poe Society, 1978. The only book to focus on Poe's crucial revisions.

Ed. *Masques, Mysteries and Mastodons: A Poe Miscellany*. Baltimore: The Edgar Allan Poe Society, 2006. Essays that bring to bear recent critical approaches (several on race), as well as several reprinting important contemporaneous documents.

Fusco, Richard. "Poe and the Perfectibility of Man," *Poe Studies* 19 (1986): 1–6. Valuable for Poe's skepticism about the theme of progress in American society, a topic of considerable interest in his era.

Hayes, Kevin J. Ed. *The Cambridge Companion to Edgar Allan Poe*. Cambridge: Cambridge University Press, 2002. Chapters cover all important aspects of Poe's career, from poetic techniques, through Gothicism, race, critical outlook, comic impulses; several chapters treat important individual works.

*Poe and the Printed Word*. Cambridge: Cambridge University Press, 2000. A valuable History of the Book approach to Poe; also treats his reading.

Jacobs, Robert D. *Poe: Journalist & Critic*. Baton Rouge: Louisiana State University Press, 1969. The best single book on Poe's critical philosophies.

Kopley, Richard. Ed. *Poe's* Pym: *Critical Explorations.* Durham, NC and London: Duke University Press, 1992. Essays that offer perspectives, from important Poe scholars, on all aspects of Poe's novel.

Ljungquist, Kent P. *The Grand and the Fair: Poe's Landscape Aesthetics and Pictorial Techniques.* Potomac, Md.: Scripta Humanistica, 1994. Excellent study of Poe's works that incorporate popular landscape theories of his day.

Peeples, Scott. *Edgar Allan Poe Revisited.* New York: Twayne; London: Prentice Hall International, 1998. Fine brief biography, along with synthesis of many ideas regarding Poe's writings.

Pollin, Burton R. *Dictionary of Names and Titles in Poe's Collected Works.* New York: Da Capo Press, 1968. Helpful directory to expedite research on Poe's works.

Quinn, Arthur Hobson. *Edgar Allan Poe: A Critical Biography* [1941]. Reprinted with intro. by Shawn Rosenheim. Baltimore: The Johns Hopkins University Press, 1985. Remains the best biographical account.

Ramakrishna, D. Ed. *Perspectives on Poe.* New Delhi: APC Publications, 1996. Fine collection of essays that cover all aspects of Poe's work.

Thomas, Dwight and David K. Jackson. *The Poe Log: A Documentary Life of Edgar Allan Poe 1809–1849.* Boston: G. K. Hall, 1987. Matchless assembly of facts about Poe's life and writings. When the compilers cannot verify a fact they say so. Indispensable for anyone interested in Poe.

Vines, Lois Davis. Ed. *Poe Abroad: Influences, Reputation, Affinities.* Iowa City: University of Iowa Press, 1999. Essays that attest Poe's popularity throughout the world, from his day to ours.

Whalen, Terence. *Edgar Allan Poe and the Masses: The Political Economy of Literature in Antebellum America.* Princeton: Princeton University Press, 1999. The best recent charting of Poe's financial/literary status, with the most sensible treatment of Poe and race.

Wilbur, Richard. "Poe and the Art of Suggestion," *University of Mississippi Studies in English,* n.s. 3 (1982): 1–13. An updating/expansion of views on Poe's achievements in symbolic writing.

# Index

# The Cambridge Introductions to . . .

## AUTHORS

*Edgar Allan Poe* Benjamin F. Fisher

*Jane Austen* Janet Todd

*Samuel Beckett* Ronan McDonald

*Walter Benjamin* David Ferris

*Joseph Conrad* John Peters

*Jacques Derrida* Leslie Hill

*Emily Dickinson* Wendy Martin

*George Eliot* Nancy Henry

*T. S. Eliot* John Xiros Cooper

*Michel Foucault* Lisa Downing

*William Faulkner* Theresa M. Towner

*F. Scott Fitzgerald* Kirk Curnutt

*Robert Frost* Robert Faggen

*Nathaniel Hawthorne* Leland S. Person

*Zora Neale Hurston* Lovalerie King

*James Joyce* Eric Bulson

*Herman Melville* Kevin J. Hayes

*Sylvia Plath* Jo Gill

*Ezra Pound* Ira Nadel

*Shakespeare* Emma Smith

*Harriet Beecher Stowe* Sarah Robbins

*Mark Twain* Peter Messent

*Walt Whitman* M. Jimmie Killingsworth

*Virginia Woolf* Jane Goldman

*W. B. Yeats* David Holdeman

## TOPICS

*The American Short Story* Martin Scofield

*Creative Writing* David Morley

*Early English Theatre* Janette Dillon

*English Theatre, 1660–1900* Peter Thomson

*Francophone Literature* Patrick Corcoran

*Modernism* Pericles Lewis

*Modern Irish Poetry* Justin Quinn

*Narrative* (second edition) H. Porter Abbott

*The Nineteenth-Century American Novel* Gregg Crane

*Postcolonial Literatures* C. L. Innes

*Russian Literature* Caryl Emerson

*Shakespeare's Comedies* Penny Gay

*Shakespeare's History Plays* Warren Chernaik

*Shakespeare's Tragedies* Janette Dillon

*The Short Story in English* Adrian Hunter

*Theatre Studies* Christopher Balme

*Tragedy* Jennifer Wallace